on track ...

The Police

every album, every song

Peter Braidis

sonicbondpublishing.com

Sonicbond Publishing Limited
www.sonicbondpublishing.co.uk
Email: info@sonicbondpublishing.co.uk

First Published in the United Kingdom 2024
First Published in the United States 2024

British Library Cataloguing in Publication Data:
A Catalogue record for this book is available from the British Library

Typeset in ITC Garamond Std & ITC Avant Garde Gothic
Printed and bound in England

Graphic design and typesetting: Full Moon Media

Follow us on social media:
Twitter: https://twitter.com/SonicbondP
Instagram: www.instagram.com/sonicbondpublishing_/
Facebook: www.facebook.com/SonicbondPublishing/

Linktree QR code:

Foreword

Rock trios have always been something of a special breed. In the late 1960s, power trios such as Cream, The Jimi Hendrix Experience and the James Gang emerged. The 1970s had its own roster of trios and The Police were one that emerged in the decade, featuring three chaps named Sting, Stewart Copeland and Andy Summers (Summers replaced initial guitar player Henry Padovani, although the band were very briefly a four-piece with both guitarists). The Police covered an awful lot of ground with their musical scope, incorporating reggae, new wave, punk (in the early days of the band), world music, rock and pop. To me and many others, it was quite fascinating to hear the development from the scorching blast of 'Fall Out' in 1977 to the haunting soundscapes of 'Tea in the Sahara' in 1983. The Police never settled for the same sound and continued to experiment and diversify throughout each album and tour.

The consistency of the band's initial existence from 1977-1986 was nothing short of amazing, all the more so because they truly loathed one another a lot of the time as the years went on, especially Sting and Copeland. By 1986, it was over.

Somehow, a glorious reunion tour finally happened in 2007-08 that is unlikely to occur ever again, most likely writing the final chapter on the band's career. The demise of The Police saddened me greatly at the time, but looking back from a distance, I can now see that they may have packed it in at the right time, with five stellar albums in a career that was only for a total of nine years. This band's music has lived on ever since the breakup and their songs have been used in countless films, television shows and commercials and have also been covered by a wide variety of artists.

The reason for this book is simple. It is to discuss each song from each album by The Police and how that music was crafted and created. All the numerous B-sides and rare non-album tracks will also be discussed.

A very special thanks goes out to Stephen Lambe for allowing me to write this book, as well as to Gordon, Stewart and Andy for the wonderful music through the years. I also want to mention Pete Sarubbi for his constant friendship, his similar obsession for music and the numerous concerts we have seen over the years. The same thanks go to Sue Tracey, Pat Dooley, Doug Johnson, Wendy Stokes and many others. And to Rachel – I've loved no one more than you and we've always shared a bond for the music of The Police, so now you're a part of it.

Most importantly, as I finished writing this book, my best friend Craig Kline passed away after a valiant battle with cancer. I've seen over 450 concerts or so and at least half were with Craig, including The Police and a few Sting shows. This book is solely dedicated to Craig.

Peter Braidis
February 2024

on track ...
The Police

Contents

Musical Careers Before The Police 7
The Early Days 10
Early Police Recordings 13
The Formation Of The Classic Lineup 15
Outlandos D'Amour (1978) 17
Reggatta De Blanc (1979)...26
Zenyatta Mondatta (1980)...36
Ghost In The Machine (1981)..48
Synchronicity (1983)...65
The Police Hiatus And The Guys Fly Solo 85
The 1986 Amnesty International Concerts And Failed Studio Album.............88
The Reunion Era 90
Coda. Summers V Sting? 93
The Police Compilation Albums 94
The Police Live Albums 99
The Police Box Sets 101
Strontium 90 Albums 104
The Police Video Releases..108
The Police On The Road..115
References and Bibliography 127

Musical Careers Before The Police

Sting

Born Gordon Matthew Thomas Sumner on 2 October 1951 in Wallsend, Northumberland, England, Sting was the oldest of four children and grew up near the shipyards. Sting did begin college but left after one term and took jobs as a bus conductor, building labourer and tax collector.

After that, it was back to college at Northern Counties College of Education, where he received a qualifications to be a teacher. Sting began playing music on the weekends during this time and became a decent bassist. Among the acts he played with were the Phoenix Jazzmen, Newcastle Big Band and Last Exit. It was with Last Exit that Sting first made his mark musically, and they achieved significant local success from 1974-76 but found breaking out of the Newcastle scene difficult. They managed to release a single in 1975 called 'Whispering Voices' on a small indie label, but it went unnoticed. A cassette was also released in 1975 called *First from Last Exit,* but that too went nowhere. The material was very good, though and Carol Wilson, who was the head of Richard Branson's publishing company, offered them a contract while Virgin Records put up the money for a demo recording. The demo was pitched to a variety of labels and some showed interest. However, no deal materialized because few knew how to market a band that mixed of jazz, pop and rock.

The band relocated to London in early 1977, but after only a few gigs, some of the band moved back to Newcastle, unable to adjust. Sting and keyboardist Gerry Richardson stayed in London. Richardson would become soul singer Billy Ocean's musical director and enjoyed success whilst Sting hitched his wagon to a new punk rock act called The Police that Stewart Copeland was putting together, which he saw as his way to get some sort of musical career going before it was too late.

Stewart Copeland

The son of a CIA agent named Miles Copeland Jr., Stewart Copeland was born in Alexandria, Virginia in the US on 16 July 1952.During his early years, Stewart's family moved several times around the middle east. It wasn't until the age of twelve that Stewart started playing the drums and in the late 1960s, he moved to the UK to attend boarding school in Somerset.

Stewart attended college back in the US at Cal-Berkley University. However, Copeland eventually returned to the UK for a career in music and became a road manager for the progressive rock outfit Curved Air. He subsequently joined the band in late 1974 until their breakup in late 1976. He appeared on the albums *Midnight Wire* (1975) and *Airborne* (1976) and on the latter album, he also co-wrote a few songs. The albums sold poorly, but they marked Stewart's recording debut. Curved Air disbanded in late 1976.

Of course, we know Stewart then formed what became The Police in 1977, but he also recorded under the pseudonym Klark Kent. Although this material was recorded at the same time as The Police were active, Copeland hit the charts before The Police ever did, with the single 'Don't Care' reaching 48 on the UK singles charts in 1978 several months before The Police charted with 'Can't Stand Losing You'. A mini-LP called *Klark Kent* surfaced in 1980, with Stewart playing all the instruments. It was the same snappy and goofy new wave that the single had been but didn't attract much attention.

In 1978, Stewart (as Klark Kent) appeared on the BBC's *Top of the Pops* and Sting, Andy and a few others appeared on stage with him in masks playing 'Don't Care'. Sting was a gorilla and Andy was Leonid Brezhnev. Also on stage in masks were road manager Kim Turner and former Curved Air drummer Florian Pilkington-Miksa. So, rather bizarrely, the first TV appearance by The Police was wearing strange masks and miming to a Stewart solo song.

Andy Summers

Andy was considerably older than Sting and Stewart and was born on 31 December 1942 in Poulton-le-Fylde, Lancashire, England. Summers and his family relocated to Bournemouth and it was here where he began an interest in playing musical instruments, including piano and guitar. He excelled on the guitar by playing jazz and started playing clubs by age sixteen.

He played with Zoot Money's Big Roll Band and appeared on the albums *It Should've Been Me* (1965) and *Zoot!* (1966) before the band evolved into a psychedelic-rock outfit called Dantalian's Chariot, who issued an album called *Chariot Rising* to little interest. Andy would then join the experimental jazz rock/psychedelic/progressive rock outfit Soft Machine for a little while and toured the US with the band in the summer of 1968, including gigs opening for the Jimi Hendrix Experience, with whom they shared the same management. Within a few months, however, Summers would move on.

Later that same summer, Andy became a member of Eric Burdon and the New Animals. His old pal Zoot Money came along with him. This lineup didn't last long, but did record the double album *Love Is,* which came out in December 1968. A highlight on the album was a nine-minute cover of the Traffic song 'Coloured Rain', which featured a scorching four-minute guitar solo from Summers. The album also produced a top 40 hit in the UK with a cover of Johnny Cash's 'Ring of Fire'.

A main reason this lineup dissolved so quickly was due to a frightening Japanese tour in the autumn of 1968, which had been delayed a few months. To recuperate money the promoters had lost due to the delay, they kidnapped the band's manager and forced him to write a promissory note of £25,000 at gunpoint. Unbeknownst to the band, the promoters were members of the Yakuza (the Japanese mob). The yakuza did release the manager but told him and the Animals to flee the country by the next day or they'd be killed. The band, management and road crew promptly fled the country and left all their equipment behind.

Andy then moved to Los Angeles, studied classical guitar and graduated from Cal-Northridge University with a degree, returning to London in 1972. Summers then went into sessions and occasional touring with a wide variety of musical artists such as Kevin Coyne, David Essex, Neil Sedaka and Joan Armatrading. With Armatrading, he appeared on her 1975 album *Back to the Night,* playing lead guitar on her classic 'Steppin' Out'. Sessions continued, but it was that fateful time in 1977 when Mike Howlett of Gong asked Summers to stand in on guitar in Howlett's new act Strontium 90, which would also include Sting and Stewart Copeland, that Andy's career path would project upward.

The Early Days

In the year of 1976, punk rock was the talk of the music world amongst both fans and critics. And many critics trying to be hip, quickly latched on to this allegedly new form of music, declaring older acts like The Rolling Stones, Pink Floyd, Jethro Tull and the like as 'Dinosaur Rock'. However, it was very exaggerated by the media as many of the 'dinosaur' acts were putting out hugely successful albums and filling concert venues even during the height of punk. While many punk acts couldn't legitimately play a note and just screamed their way through poorly written songs, there is some truth in saying that quite a few of these bands acts could actually play, write and sing rather well. In many cases, these acts hid that fact behind a three-chord approach and didn't want to be caught actually playing well or – god forbid – putting in a real guitar solo. But by the late 1970s, it was quite clear that the brief chaos of what punk started as had faded to a large degree.

In his Police Diaries, published in 2023, Copeland discussed the atmosphere in London in 1976 and how it affected him:

> And this was soooo not dance music as hitherto known. The kids were electric but there was a similar voltage of outrage from all of our fancy friends. The prog cognoscenti were coughing, spluttering and sulking on the perimeter. There were no triplets! Only two chords! That's not singing, it's shouting! But Ian's got a connection with the dance floor. Everybody in show business is searching for the Next Big Thing and we were looking at it right there. The suits and the short hair were like a nightmare version of The Man that hippies were congenitally opposed to. The revenge of straight people returned as electrified zombies high on glue rather than pot! Those kids were an insult to everything that my band stood for, but dang! I felt like I was on their side.

Copeland began to look for a band to reflect this new zeitgeist. He knew he would struggle to sing from behind his kit, so he began looking for a guitarist and bassist, on the bassist that one of them would have to sing.

So, around the autumn of 1976, Stewart Copeland met Gordon Sumner, who was playing with Last Exit. Sumner, who was nicknamed Sting due to a particularly hideous black and yellow striped sweater that he wore, was intrigued by Copeland's musical knowledge and enthusiasm. Sting knew that the jazz rock format wasn't exactly going to pay the bills, so he asked Copeland what he had in mind musically and became intrigued, deciding hitch his hopes on Stewart and his new band. Sting but did realize that it was a possible springboard towards getting noticed if they could pull it together. However, a guitarist was needed and Copeland remembered a fellow he had come across who was a native of Corsica named Henry Padovani.

Padovani wasn't a brilliant, flashy player, but he knew the basic chords and attitude of punk, resulting in Copeland inviting him into the band. Stewart remembered to Hugh Fielder in *La Historia Bandito*:

He (Padovani) knew a few chords and he was really enthusiastic and when he'd had his hair cut and stuff, he really looked the part. I mean, he could play guitar better than I could and I could play guitar better than Joe Strummer ... well, in those days. So I reckoned he'd be OK, but I didn't figure Sting would see it that way ...

Sting agreed to accept Padovani into the band, but not without some reluctance. Padovani recalled in his book *Secret Police Man* that he and Stewart donned shades and leather, while Sting showed up to the first practice in jeans with his wife and baby:

When Sting arrived with his baby in a travel cot (Sting and his then-wife Frances had recently had their first child, Joe), we'd adopted the pose of dangerous rockers, silent and moody. Sting was wearing dungarees. He must have thought we looked like idiots.

Sting wasn't a beneficiary of a particularly great childhood, living in a shipbuilding area of England known as Wallsend, but he did have aspirations of doing more than what he saw the grizzled, hard-working men doing each day just to survive. Sting attributed the beginning of music in his life to a four-stringed guitar that had been left behind by a family friend: 'As soon as I saw that guitar, I realized I'd found my route out – my best friend', adding 'I didn't speak for four years, I just played the guitar. I saved up for the other strings'. Being so used to playing four strings, it is no wonder that he became such a fantastic bassist.

Sting learned to like the songs that Stewart had come up with and he soon started offering up his own songs. However, according to Padovani in his book *Secret Police Man*:

Stewart stopped him each time. He said, 'Sting, you still don't get it. Write something like 'my job is a heap of shit and I'm going to smash everything up!' *THAT* we can play'. I could see Sting seething inside and then he'd play at three times his normal speed and Stewart loved that.

This is how songs like 'Landlord', 'Dead End Job' and 'Visions of the Night' began to surface.

The Police had some songs, but they had no gigs and no money. It was Stewart's brother Miles who came to the rescue, getting the band some shows supporting New York-based punk singer Cherry Vanilla. Cherry couldn't afford to bring her band to the UK, so Miles offered The Police as backup. They received a whopping £15 a night. And the guys also got to open the gigs as The Police, with shows beginning on 1 March 1977 at Newport Stowaway in South Wales. The band played ten songs in seventeen minutes at their first show – now that's punk rock!

The other influence on the band was reggae. Originating from the Caribbean, this musical form had grown in stature since the arrival of the first wave of immigrants in the late 1940s. By the 1970s, with the commercial success of Bob Marley and home-grown British acts like Steel Pulse, it had made its mark on British culture. Furthermore, unlike progressive or jazz rock, it had credibility. Sting told *The Breakfast Club* in 2018:

For me it was homage to something that I loved. I was brought up in England in the '50s and '60s, and we had a very influential West Indian community, so I grew up with calypso and ska music, and Blue Beat. And then when Bob Marley came to England it was very revolutionary to me because he turned rock music on its head. The importance of the bass —as a bass player, that was hugely influential to me — the way the drums are played is completely different. And then Marley's philosophy, his spiritual message, his political message was very powerful. For me, it wasn't cultural appropriation, it was homage to something that I loved and I still love.

In February 1977, The Police had entered the recording studio to cut their debut single and thus began, in an inauspicious way, the recording career of a band that would eventually have massive worldwide success.

Early Police Recordings

'Fall Out' (Copeland)

Recorded on 12 February 1977 and issued on 1 May 1977, the debut single from The Police was a two-minute and three-second blast of rocking, catchy punk rock. The song was recorded before the band's live debut and had cost a borrowed £150 to make. The track was written by Copeland and Stewart played the rhythm guitar parts in addition to his usual drum duties due to Padovani's inability to stay in time. Padovani laid down the lead guitar and Sting handled the dual roles of bass and vocals. 'Fall Out' is a fun, energetic tune that does all it needs to do. The musicality was obvious, however. It was clear that this was no garage band.

The song's grimy power chords blast away, the chorus is catchy and the rhythm drives hard. It's also fun hearing Sting shout 'Henri!' as Padovani gets ready to rip into his guitar solo. In the liner notes to the 1993 box set *Message in a Box*, Sting discussed the song:

> This was one of the first songs Stewart played me. What they [the songs] lacked in sophistication, they made up for in energy. I just went along with them and sang them as hard as I could. No, it wasn't false punk. I mean, what's a real punk? Our first record was entirely a tribute to Stewart's energy and focus. The band wouldn't have happened without him.

'Fall Out' would not chart initially when it was issued on Illegal Records, the label set up by Stewart's older brother Miles and the band's then-manager Paul Milligan. When reissued in 1979 after the band became a success, the song would reach 47 on the UK singles charts. The cover for the sleeve had the band looking very punk indeed and the single would be reviewed by Rolling Stones frontman Mick Jagger for the popular music magazine *Sounds*. Stewart later said on the *Message In A Box* liner notes:

> It was a heartfelt lyric, all about a personal disinclination to follow the styles of my peers. It was the first song that we rehearsed as The Police and also our first recording. We recorded it in a tiny studio and it was one of the rare instances in which I got to play the guitar. On this track and on 'Nothing Achieving', I played the main guitar tracks and Henry Padovani did the solo in the middle. When Andy joined the group, my guitar went back in the closet.

'Nothing Achieving' (Copeland)

This was the B-side to 'Fall Out' and was another Copeland tune; a short, punked out number that had a darker edge than 'Fall Out'. Though the song is credited to Stewart alone, his brother Ian and Sting helped re-write parts of it to make it work better. The song is even shorter than the A-side was, clocking in at just 1:56, which certainly stuck to the punk aesthetic.

The song does rock quite a bit with aggression and anger. Once again, Stewart plays the rhythm guitar parts, with Padovani playing the lead. The drumming is way above what anyone would expect from a 'punk' song in terms of technique and Sting elevates the song even more with his vocal. Padovani lays down a pretty lethal solo and although it's a little ugly and off-kilter, it works just fine for what the song requires. One can't help but wonder just how long Stewart and Sting could've lasted playing this style of music. Stewart was quoted in the boxset as saying:

My brother Ian actually wrote the words for this song, with changes by Sting and me. Very dark, very hostile. It was a major step forward when Sting started writing the songs. I had a zillion guitar riffs like this, but Sting actually had something useful to say about the world.

'Clowns Revenge' (Kristina)
Incorrectly listed at times as 'Clouds in Venice', this song was performed live in the earliest days by the band when they were short of material. There are several concert recordings of this number; a hyper rocker with an aggressive drum shuffle and blocky punk power chords with some single-note riffing.

The song was written by Stewart's former Curved Air bandmate and future wife Sonja Kristina (they were married from 1982 to 1991). The best recordings of this track are from shows on 6 March 1977 in London and the final show as a four-piece on 5 August 1977 in Mont-de-Marsan, France.

'Night At The Grand Hotel' (Sting)
Another song from the early, early days of The Police, this particular tune was played fairly often in 1977 concerts. This song is sometimes also listed as 'Night in the Grand Hotel'. There are a number of live recordings of this song, which Last Exit had also performed, although the Last Exit version was more of a slick pop-rocker with the same chords.

The way The Police played this song was as a four-on-the-floor power chord rocker with a 1950s vibe that sounded like a heavy Chuck Berry song. There were also some stop-start parts that sounded like an Eddy Cochran tune. Not surprisingly, the song moved quickly and wasn't too imaginative.

The Formation Of The Classic Lineup

In the spring of 1977 an aggregation called Strontium 90 came into existence a few months after the 'Fallout' single had been released. Mike Howlett was the bass player in Gong, a French/British/Australian progressive rock act formed in Paris in 1967, which later had some significant success in Europe. Howlett joined Gong in 1973 and played with the band until 1977, when he decided to depart. It was around this time that Howlett decided to try and form a new band with Sting and Stewart; they began rehearsing to play at a Gong reunion gig that would feature a variety of current and ex-Gong members playing with their current outfits.

For this gig, Howlett added Andy Summers who was playing guitar for Kevin Ayers. He was a very experienced guitarist who was tiring of being a sideman and was excited at the prospect of playing in something new, even if it was only temporary. The concert took place on 28 May and Strontium 90 (named after the chemical Strontium, which is atomic number 38. As Strontium 90 is radioactive and can cause major damage to the human body, especially bone) blew through their set, which was pretty propulsive, loud rock unlike most of the trippy stuff that was played that day by the other acts. Was greatness detected by the audience? No, but Summers felt there was something there and the next morning, he saw Sting at breakfast and said, 'It seems to me I should join The Police'. He told Stewart the same thing later on.

Andy later told *Mojo*: 'I thought, this band is nothing, the songs are shitty, and why would I want to do this? Me, still embracing bourgeois values like wanting to be able to play your fucking instrument. It was ridiculous for me, wasn't it?' Nonetheless, he kept nagging the boys to join and finally, he did. The Police played their first gig as a quartet at the Music Machine in London on 25 July 1977. Summers did not enjoy playing with Padovani and asked the band to remove Padovani, but out of loyalty, Sting and Stewart said no. The group performed one more time as a quartet at the *Mont de Marsan Punk Festival* on 5 August in France.

After an attempt at recording sessions, with former Velvet Underground member John Cale producing, failed in late August 1977, Sting and Stewart agreed that Padovani was technically lacking and had to go. Henry took it well and told *Mojo*: 'If Andy hadn't arrived, the band would have died'.

Summers, however, insists that he wasn't solely responsible for why that move was made, but he also said that he wasn't just going to accept anything less than what was needed for the band to excel and said in the same article:

This is the stuff groups are made from: conflict, desire, betrayal and strategies that Machiavelli would be proud of. I saw that I could go on forever as a good sideman, but in me, the strongest need is to be an artist and a supreme musician. As far as I'm concerned the group didn't start until I joined.

The first gig as a trio with Summers was on 18 August at a club called Rebecca's in Birmingham. The band largely played short, quick-paced shows that left no room to breathe. Despite how unusual it was for a 'punk' band to be a trio, they were still very much a part of that scene at this juncture. Of course, the goal all along was NOT to be a punk band but to use punk as a springboard that would propel their music into further reaches of genre. And the gambit paid off, though it took a while and in the meantime, there was a lot of scrounging for gigs, food and affordable living conditions. This was especially difficult for Sting, as he had a newborn baby boy and wife.

From late 1977 to early 1978, the guys were able to make some money by recording and touring with German experimentalist/keyboardist/composer Eberhard Schoener. Summers had played on a solo album by Deep Purple keyboard wizard Jon Lord called *Sarabande* in 1975, which featured an orchestra conducted by Schoener, hence the connection. The reason the band got involved with Schoener is because Summers had already agreed to record with him in advance, as well as play some gigs, so Sting and Stewart came along and also participated in the music the German had in mind. The band worked on three of his albums, including *Video Magic* and *Flashback*. Sting sings in an ultra-high register in this project, more so than at any time with The Police. Interesting songs include a very electronically-driven piece called 'Why Don't You Answer' from 1978 that sounds like Sting meeting up with Kraftwerk on a dance floor. The Police did several TV appearances with Schoener in Germany and Sting's voice attracted a lot of attention.

In February 1978, the band was desperate enough for cash that they accepted an offer to do a TV advert for Wrigley's Spearmint chewing gum and they all dyed their hair blonde for the shoot because that's what was requested. The commercial was filmed but never aired. It was directed by the legendary Tony Scott, later to direct such films as *Top Gun*, *The Hunger*, *Enemy of the State*, *Crimson Tide* and *True Romance*.

Within a few months things started happening for the band under the guidance of Miles Copeland; thus chewing gum commercials, posing as punks and backing German experimental composers would be left behind and the true recording career of the band would begin.

Outlandos D'Amour (1978)

Personnel:
Sting: bass, lead vocals, 'butt' piano, harmonica
Andy Summers: guitars, backing vocals, piano, spoken word
Stewart Copeland: drums, percussion, backing vocals
Released: 2 November 1978
Recorded: Surrey Sound Studios (London, UK)
Producer: The Police
Engineer: Nigel Gray
Cover Design: Les May
Highest chart position: UK: 6, US: 23, Canada: 22, Australia: 15

The Police issued their debut album in the fall of 1978 and immediately hit the road to promote it, as management did not want to rely solely on reviews, radio and print media. The sessions for the album took six months, but that was largely because they couldn't always book time and were playing gigs. The budget wasn't exactly excessive either, as they borrowed around £1,500 from their manager, Miles. Whenever Miles visited the studio, he could be harsh, but after hearing 'Roxanne' his mind was changed so much so that he took it to A&M Records and asked the label to issue the song as a one-off single. The label agreed, but the single failed to chart in the UK when released on 1 April 1978. A&M, however, were interested in another single.

'Can't Stand Losing You' was next up later that year on 14 August 1978. The song became a minor hit, reaching 42 in the UK and leading A&M to green-light a full album. The song did stir up some controversy as the sleeve for the single had an image of Copeland about to hang himself. The BBC had issues with the song just because of the cover, and, ever the opportunist, Miles Copeland used this as publicity, which in turn helped the single chart. Reviews were mixed, with *Rolling Stone* accusing the band of being pretend punks, while reviews in the UK were generally more positive, *Sounds* calling it a 'a distinctive and mostly enjoyable first album'. But of course, the album was quickly reappraised. In fact, the album is now ranked at 428 on the *Rolling Stone 500 Greatest Albums of All-Time* list and at 38 on that same magazine's list of the *100 Best Debut Albums of All-Time*.

There are some unusual tracks on the album and that would be the case with more than one Police record, but those moments are also often bizarre fun, often in dark, morbid ways. Miles Copeland wanted the album to be called *Police Brutality,* but A&M wisely vetoed that idea. Copeland then suggested the title that was ultimately chosen, which was *Outlandos d'Amour*. Roughly translated from French, it means 'Outlaws of Love'.

The Police were not a success right out of the gate. It wasn't until a few months into 1979 that the album itself began selling and that was due to 'Roxanne' cracking the US singles charts in February and ultimately making the top 40 (it also achieved a top 40 placing in Canada). In the UK, the single was reissued in April, where it soared to number twelve while 'Can't Stand Losing You' went all the way to number two with 'So Lonely' hitting the UK top ten as well in 1980.

Outlandos d'Amour would ultimately peak at number six on the UK album charts in October 1979, charting a total of 38 weeks and number 23 in the US, where it also went platinum and charted for an amazing 63 weeks total. The album would also attain platinum status in the UK a year later.

When The Police first toured the US in the fall of 1978, nobody in the States had ever heard of the band and it was one of the many strategies by Miles Copeland that panned out brilliantly. Miles' brother Ian was an agent in the US and together they came up with the idea of the band touring the Northeast in a van to keep costs down. They would play college towns and create a bond with a younger audience who could lay claim to 'discovering' the band when they broke. The band would stop by college radio stations to chat and score some airplay and then play the gig that night. It was tedious, arduous and exhausting, but it would pay off.

The first US show was in New York at the infamous club CBGB's on 20 October 1978 and the second show was around 2:30 A.M. that same night at that club. The band had actually landed off the plane that same day carrying their instruments as luggage and then played the two concerts. The evening went well and over the next month, they travelled up and down the East Coast with their instruments in that Ford Econoline van. On this tour, they played 23 gigs in 27 days and usually made around £140 ($200 US) a concert. To say they weren't exactly staying at the best motels and eating the best food would be an understatement. Kim Turner, who by now was co-managing the band with Miles, shared the driving duties and was basically the band's 'crew' – quite humble beginnings indeed.

'Next To You' (Sting)

As Stewart's drums pound the intro, it's clear that 'Next to You' rocks. Combining a punk aesthetic with infectious hooks, this power pop song is a wild ride in 2:52 minutes. It's proof positive that The Police could rock out with the best of them. Copeland uses toms and his ride cymbal and Summers has gritty muted chords in the verses, while the guitars chime in with chords during the choruses. Sting sounds great vocally, although his bass playing gets somewhat lost in the mix. The angst of the lyrics was something a lot of guys could relate to, and there are some simple, but effective lines used to express this frustration.

The other members of the band wanted Sting to sing something more disturbing involving a gun, but he refused to write such banal lyrics and it was the right move. Summers also has a snarling slide guitar solo, which cuts right to the bone. Copeland actually felt the solo was too close to a classic rock sound, but it's an awesome example of the diversity of Andy's playing and would surprise a lot of people who came to The Police late in their catalogue.

'So Lonely' (Sting)

Here is one of Sting's finest lyrics and most distinctive vocal performances. 'So Lonely' humorously examines takes a look at the pains of being alone. There are so many great lines in this song that exemplify how great a lyricist Mr. Sumner already was even at this early stage of his career. Each line is a mixture of pain and dark, self-deprecating humour that anyone can relate to.

Of course, the idea that someone who looks like Sting would be sitting alone on a Saturday night seems farfetched, but at some point, even he must've had his heart ripped out or felt isolated. Sting acknowledged in his book *Lyrics by Sting* that the song began with a song for his previous band Last Exit and that he had the lyrics already, but 'then grafted shamelessly' onto the chords for Bob Marley's 'No Woman, No Cry'. Well, yes, you can definitely hear that, but it works so well, does it really matter? The subject matter works in tandem with the track's musical juxtaposition; the verses lean more towards a reggae-inspired sound, while the verses light up with explosive drumming and jarring guitar chords. Sting recognized this when he said, in *Lyrics By Sting*:

> This kind of musical juxtaposition, the lilting rhythm of the verses separated by monolithic slabs of straight rock and roll, pleased the hell out of me. That we could achieve it effortlessly just added to the irony of a song about misery being sung so joyously.

And indeed, there it is. This upbeat, buoyant song about desolate loneliness and rejection worked like a charm. The vocal starts just a second into the song after a brief drum intro and the listener is sucked in right away. Sting's vocals are double-tracked on the last half of the verses and Andy lays down a pretty snarling solo that continues as Sting and Stewart evolve the rhythm. At the 3:30 mark, the song breaks down into Sting repeating the 'I feel so low', which was clearly destined for extension on the live stage. And does it even matter that the band sings the title over 50 times? Nope!

'So Lonely' initially failed as a single, as previously mentioned, but it was reissued in 1980 and made the UK top ten on the singles charts, peaking at number six and being certified silver, charting for ten weeks.

There was a music video made for the song that year, which saw the band on the streets of Hong Kong and in the subways of Tokyo – this had nothing to do with the song whatsoever, it's just where they were on tour at the time. This clip was never shown on MTV. In the UK, some listeners misheard the title as 'Sue Lawley', who was a well-known presenter on TV on the BBC. I also think there's a potential Weird Al Yankovic parody in there called 'Salami'.

'Roxanne' (Sting)

The song about a prostitute that became the breakthrough for the band, 'Roxanne', is indeed the stuff of legend. As already mentioned, the song was their major label debut on A&M Records but failed to chart initially in 1978. The song scored in the US and Canada, though, making the Top 40 in both countries in early 1979, reaching number 32 in the US. Thus, the song was reissued in the UK in April and became a hit, reaching number twelve on the singles charts.

After Stewart opens the song on hi-hat and Andy Summers comes in on guitar with those now-famous opening chords, we hear an odd piano note and a laugh from Sting. Why? Well, it was because Sting tripped and fell backwards in the studio, landing his behind on the piano, and they left that note in as well as his chuckle.

Sting was inspired to write the song in 1977 when the band were touring in France and he observed prostitutes in the street. He then conceived of the idea of a man who had fallen in love with one of the ladies of the evening. A poster for the old film *Cyrano de Bergerac* was in the foyer of the hotel and the main female character in that film was named Roxanne, thus the inspiration for the title. In fact, Summers remembered the origins of the track very well in a later interview with *Classic Rock*:

> We were supposed to do this shitty little gig with The Damned, and we'd driven to Paris from Holland in my Citroen Dyane 6. The night before, we all went our separate ways and Sting was wandering around, looking at all the hookers.

The band arrived at the venue only to be told the show was cancelled and that The Damned, according to Summers, 'had pissed off back to England'. Sting initially wrote the song as a bossa nova, which was going to work in 1978 (although it might have on a latter-day Sting solo album). Andy added:

> We started playing around with it and came up with something where I was able to play four-in-the-bar, Stewart put that slight reggae thing on and Sting changed where he put the bass beats. We worked it up in one afternoon.

Summers also stated that:

> We were a bit embarrassed about 'Roxanne' because this was the raging punk scene, where everything was at furious speed. And we had this kind of ballad. But Miles thought it was great. He took it to A&M, and they wanted to release it. It didn't become a hit at first, but a few people noticed it, and I think it was John Pidgeon from *Melody Maker* who wrote a great review of the song.

Of course, the BBC were not thrilled that the song was about a prostitute, but nothing about the song was salacious or slimy. Summers mentioned the importance of the song and how it broke them in the States:

Originally, it was picked up by a radio station in Texas. From there, it went to WBCN-FM in Boston and this disc jockey called Oedipus started to play it in heavy rotation. Then the song picked up and everyone started to play it. We didn't have a record deal in the States, but because of 'Roxanne' and this heavy rotation in Boston, A&M in America came to see us. They got it pretty quick and signed us to an American deal. And it all started to unfold quickly from there.

There was a music video for the song that MTV played, once they took to the airwaves in 1981, and the clip was also shown on standard American television. There are actually two different versions, with one showing the band seemingly at a sound check while the other has the infamous 'red light'.

'Roxanne' was also famously sung by comedian/actor Eddie Murphy in a memorable scene in the hit film *48 Hours* in 1982, and it was the song the band chose to play at the 2007 Grammy Awards when they reintroduced themselves to the world just prior to their enormously successful reunion tour of 2007-08. 'Roxanne' is in both the Grammy Hall of Fame and the Rock and Roll Hall of Fame, and rightfully so.

'Hole In My Life' (Sting)
This song is another with a vaguely reggae sound, although the band funk it up a little and Sting's bass playing is prominent. Andy Summers plays a descending guitar line with minor chords and it is he who plays the piano parts that we hear here and there. Stewart's drumming is excellent, with lots of crashing snare drum, cymbals and creative fills.

The lyrics express the dark reality and humour that pervades the album, thus, it stays consistent with the twisted themes the band explores throughout. The song largely stays in one mode, only changing for the bridge with Sting pondering: 'There's something missing from my life, Cuts me open like a knife, It leaves me vulnerable, I have this disease, I shake like an incurable, God help me please'. The whole song is pretty dismal lyrically, yet the perky way the band plays the song is another one of those clever juxtapositions.

'Hole in My Life' does go on way too long (just shy of five minutes) and it is a bit repetitive. Nonetheless, this was played at most concerts in the band's career and the group would always do a stop/start, letting the audience shout back.

'Peanuts' (Copeland/Sting)
Here's a spitfire of a rocker with the band slamming over-exposed celebrities, which was a very punk thing to do. The song was largely about one celebrity in particular (as Sting has often said) – Rod Stewart. Sting was commenting on Rod going from rowdy rocker with The Faces to dating models, going down the easy listening route and being in the papers and on TV every minute.

Musically speaking, the song is arguably The Police's most powerful, as it is an out-and-out rocker with heavy power chords and ferocious drumming. Summers also delivers a wicked, atonal, noisy guitar solo with spit and vigour. However, being The Police, they can't help but ham things a bit, as exemplified by the odd, squonking saxophone break.

The opening verse has Sting on the attack: 'It's all a game, You're not the same, Your famous name, The price of fame'. This is not exactly complimentary and it gets worse from there when we hit the pre-chorus: 'Oh no, try to liberate me, I said oh no, Stay and irritate me, I said oh no, Try to elevate me, I said oh no, just a fallen hero'. Let's just say that Sting was pretty disappointed with his subject.

Whether Sting later became what he was railing against is open to debate ...

The track includes a snippet of the song 'The Peanut Seller', which is a Latina tune popularised by bandleader Stan Kenton, which was used on a famous TV advert in the UK for peanuts in the 1970s.

'Can't Stand Losing You' (Sting)
And now we come to another classic and one of the album's hit singles. Taking a morbid subject yet again but craftily making it darkly humorous, Sting turned in this gem, which was the band's first actual chart hit in the UK. While teenage suicide is no joke, this song took a sardonic look at one overreacting to a breakup by threatening to commit suicide due to the heartache of the breakup.

Musically speaking, it's back to another mix of rock/reggae/pop and Summers' use of Echoplex on his guitar gives the song a layered sound. Once again, the song has an intentionally repetitive chorus that works like a charm. In concert, the band would stretch the song out past its three-minute length by doing an improvised instrumental jam that would eventually become the song 'Reggatta de Blanc' – the title track of the second album – and ended up winning a Grammy as Best Rock Instrumental.

The band made their UK TV debut for this track as well and it is now infamous for Sting's comically goofy look with suspenders and oversized glasses. The reason he wore the glasses was due to an accident that occurred during makeup for the video in which a can of hairspray ended up sending Sting to the hospital. Sting was in a hurry to get ready for the performance as he was also filming scenes for the film *Quadrophenia* at the same time and in his haste, he accidentally sprayed himself in the eyes, which caused pain and redness. This was actually a live performance on the BBC's *Old Grey Whistle Test* on 2 October 1978, which was also Sting's birthday. There was a music video as well that was shown on European television and which MTV eventually showed in the US that was essentially the same as the 'Roxanne' clip with the red background.

When the single was reissued in June 1979, it soared all the way to number two on the UK charts where it was certified silver. It was bested only by another rather more controversial song from the Boomtown Rats with 'I Don't Like Mondays', which discussed serial killings. 'Can't Stand Losing You' would also reach the top ten in Ireland and the Netherlands. Reggae legends Steel Pulse covered this song in 1997.

'Truth Hits Everybody' (Sting)

This cut originated as a Last Exit tune called 'Truth Kills' in a different form. It's a very dark song with jarring chords and a powerful chorus. The instrumental section has chiming bells that add a haunting tone. The lyrics here are dark but also introspective, as evidenced by the opening verse:

> Sleep lay behind me like a broken ocean
> Strange waking dreams before my eyes unfold
> You lay there sleeping like an open doorway
> I stepped outside myself and felt so cold

And if you thought that was heavy, well, there's another verse with these lyrics: 'I thought about it and my dream was broken, I clutch at images like dying breath, And I don't want to make a fuss about it, The only certain thing in life is death'. This is a gripping song and it's a straightforward rocker despite the downtrodden verbiage.

Long a concert favorite, this song also had a lot of Sting adding 'woahs' at the end of each chorus, which became an integral part of Police shows. The band did a very cool new version of the song in 1983 as a B-side (more on that later) and there's also a 1981 demo of the band reworking it and also jamming for a good twenty minutes, which is well worth hearing. The song has also been covered by other musical acts such as Motion City Soundtrack, Rage and No Use for a Name.

'Born In The 50's' (Sting)

More of a conventional hard rock/pop song, 'Born in the 50's' features some sweet, fat bass lines by Sting and pounding drumming by Stewart, while Andy plays choice power chords on the verses and jangles away during the choruses. The song is both infectious and lively, but it's got some truly throwaway lyrics ('Oh, we hated our aunts and messed in our pants' isn't quite Keats, is it?) and sounds more like a B-side than anything crucial to the album, beginning a string of slightly average songs to end the album.

'Be My Girl-Sally' (Sting/Summers)

And now we arrive at the demented side of the band; this was actually a combination of a song Sting had only half-written and a warped poem by Summers called 'Sally'. But Sally was no mere woman – she was actually a blow-up sex doll.

For whatever reason, the guys actually did work on this song longer than they should have, recording it at least twice before settling on the final underdeveloped piece. The song starts with some muted guitar chords, then Sting adds a bass fill and the drums kick in and lead to the repetitive 'Won't you be my girl?' refrain.

At around 52 seconds, we get Summers reciting a poem behind an off-key piano. It's an offbeat (shall we say) piece of work and I can't help but feel a little uneasy at Andy's twisted sense of whimsy.

A musical part of this song had earlier appeared on a Strontium 90 session and was revised for use here. The fact that the band played this song live for several years is testimony to their sense of humour and their ability to not take themselves too seriously.

'Masoko Tanga' (Sting)

While this closing track showcases the chops of the band, it's basically just filler and overlong filler at that. Close to six minutes long, this instrumental goes on for far too long and doesn't deviate much. Sting's bass licks are quite effective and jazz-influenced as Stewart gets a chance to lay down a sly groove and zany fills beneath this, but the piece does eventually wear on the listener.

It is the only song on the album they never played live. The bass lines carry the melody well and Sting does sing along at times, but with no actual intelligible lyrics beyond an attempt at improvised Caribbean patois. Why the punk rocking B-side 'Dead End Job' lost out to this confusing song is a mystery, although I'd guess they just wanted to mix up styles and have some fun.

As for the meaning of the title, Sting offered this chestnut:

Masoko Tanga is an indulgent experiment in the same sort of vein (of 'Be My Girl-Sally'). It's the result of an experiment by the group and a professor of paraphysics, who is famous for putting people under hypnosis, and under hypnosis, they relive incidents from what seem to be past lives. That song I sang in a language I'd never heard; I don't know what it means.

Sting and I agree on one thing: We both don't know what it means.

Outlandos D'Amour Rarities
'Dead End Job' (Copeland/Sting/Summers)

This B-side was a tune the band played live in the early days, a punked-up rocker and one of the very first songs Sting wrote for The Police. All three band members are credited with the writing due to the musical contributions, although it should be noted that this song was actually initially recorded in 1977 with the original lineup which included Padovani.

The first session took place on 8 August 1977 when the band worked (very) briefly with John Cale as producer. The silly part with Stewart reading a newspaper wasn't on the first version, but did end up on the released version, which became the B-side and came from a session on 17 January 1978, by which point Summers was in the band.

The bass drives hard and is a difficult pattern to play, especially whilst singing. The guitars are funky and mutually aggressive, whilst Stewart's drumming is very energetic, although a bit simplistic for him. The song is a one-trick pony, however, not changing the framework once during its three and a half minutes, though it is a blast to listen to.

The guys liked this one and Summers said in the box set liner notes: 'That was the one where I did a reading from a local paper in my Lancashire voice; it was the only time I ever got a compliment from Sting on my vocals'. Copeland added:

> It was another of the really early tunes from the original setlist. I think I had been playing the riff since high school. The bass line was demanding and the other punk groups held Sting in awe because he could really hammer it. It was a song that John Cale tried to produce, but this is a later recording with Andy.

'Landlord' (Copeland-Sting)
Although this was used as a B-side for the 'Message in a Bottle' single in 1979, the song originated from the earliest days of the band in 1977 and was written by Sting after he and his girlfriend Frances were tossed out of the house that they had been renting in London by a landlord, who apparently had little sympathy for two people not coming up with the rent on time.

The version used for the B-side was a live recording at the Bottom Line in New York that took place on 4 April 1979. A studio take had also been recorded during the session for *Outlandos D'Amour* but was not used for the album largely because Miles Copeland had decided that 'Roxanne' had to go on the album and thus, 'Landlord' was evicted. The song would surface on both box sets: 1993's *Message in a Box: The Complete Recordings* and on the rarities disc *Flexible Strategies* that was included with *2019's Every Move You Make: The Studio Recordings* box.

The actual riff originated from Stewart when he was in school and he also had some lyrics, but Sting discarded those and came up with his own set that worked far better. 'Landlord' lasted for several years in the live set and its raucous nature always meant that it went down well with a live audience. The opening solo from Andy is blazing and the zig-zagging riff is explosive, as if it came from a pissed-off metal guitarist.

The chorus is all Sting with those familiar vocals and Andy also unleashes a wicked solo mixing hard rock and punk tones. Stewart careens along with speed and dexterity and it's quite blatant that this was no mere punk band playing a few chords. Throw in an AC/DC styled ending, and you have a song that takes no prisoners. Take that, Mr. Landlord!

Reggatta De Blanc (1979)

Personnel:
Sting: bass, lead vocals, backing vocals, bass synthesizer
Andy Summers: guitars, keyboards, piano
Stewart Copeland: drums, percussion, lead vocals, backing vocals, guitar on 'It's Alright For You'
Released: 2 October 1979
Recorded: Surrey Sound Studios (London, UK)
Produced by Nigel Gray and The Police
Engineer: Nigel Gray
Cover Design: Michael Ross
Highest chart position: UK: 1, US: 25, Canada: 3, Japan: 16, Germany: 16, Australia: 1

The second album from The Police was an even bigger success for the band commercially, but artistically they had to reach for a few scraps to complete the record. Some of the songs were written rather quickly, and others were dug up from the past. The album took about a month to record in actual studio time, but it was spread out over several months. In a rather odd move, the band eschewed the idea of recording with a bigger budget in a fancier studio which had been suggested by A&M Records and instead once again recorded at Surrey Sound with Nigel Gray. The budget was higher than the one accorded to the debut album but was still very low at a cost somewhere between £6,000-£9,000.

The reason that they resurrected old songs was largely down to the fact that they didn't have enough new material for a full album: 'No Time This Time' was a B-side from the *Outlandos d'Amour* sessions and was chosen as the last track on the album. 'Reggatta de Blanc' had developed during the live performances of 'Can't Stand Losing You,' and both 'Bring on the Night' and 'The Bed's Too Big Without You' had begun in the days of Last Exit.

That's not to say that this album was cobbled together from outtakes and unused ideas – quite the contrary, actually. Despite not having enough time to write properly, the band still came up with a lot of very good material and the album was a big seller, receiving very good reviews. In fact, Copeland has gone on record saying it is his favorite Police album, and *Rolling Stone* lists it at number 369 of the *500 Greatest Albums of All-Time*.

The Police went on a crazy tour to support the record, which would be documented on the home video release *Police Around the World,* in which they ventured to locales that very few, if any, rock acts had gone to before. The dates began on 17 August 1979 and concluded on 28 April 1980. Aside from the UK and North America, The Police played Europe, Japan, Australia, India and Egypt.

Reggatta de Blanc would be the first number one album for The Police in the UK (also producing a pair of number one singles as well and gaining platinum status) and made the US top 25, earning platinum sales figures and racking up 100 weeks on the charts, just shy of two solid years. The album also went platinum in Canada, France, New Zealand and Australia, among other territories. The reggae influence is even more pronounced on this record than the debut (after all, the album's title loosely translates to 'White Reggae').

The playing and mixing are far crisper compared to the debut and as there are a number of Coplenad contributions, the album keeps some of that punk and new wave edges. The album itself opens with one of the band's strongest tracks.

'Message In A Bottle' (Sting)
One of The Police's greatest songs, 'Message in a Bottle' opens the album in as good a way as they could've hoped for. The song's main guitar riff was actually intended for another song that never got finished. This song also features one of the most recognizable intros in rock history and it has been covered numerous times over the years.

In the liner notes to Sting's 2019 album *My Songs*, he stated:

I wrote the guitar riff for 'Message in a Bottle' on my black Fender Strat in the back of a noisy van heading south on an Autobahn between Düsseldorf and Nuremberg sometime in early '79. I immediately knew that I was onto something with this circular riff, starting with an arpeggiated C#9, repeated in A9, then to B9, and finally F#9, resolving back to the beginning. It took me a while to find the right lyrical subject, but after a few false starts back home in my basement in Bayswater, a story emerged from the rising and falling tide of the music of some kind of Robinson Crusoe character stranded on a desert island and throwing a hopeful bottle out to sea. The countless bottles that are washed up in response continue to be a resonant and grateful metaphor in my life, but like all great rock and roll stories, it began with a riff.

Without Andy Summers and his amazing chordal embellishments and arpeggios, the song could never have reached its zenith. Summers injected some colour and phrasing that heightened the texture, mood, drama and atmosphere, especially with the way he stretched out the main chords. The track's themes of isolation, loneliness and hopelessness are mirrored musically by the minor key.

What's especially compelling about the way Sting composed the lyrics is that it tells a story that the listener can instantly identify with and uses clever metaphors. By the third verse, this mini-movie has played out with an amazing reveal, which is actually a twist ending. The music then takes on an entirely different feel, as the main character now has hope and Sting repeats the 'sending out an S.O.S'. line while Summers adds some biting leads and Copeland brings forth brilliant percussion and drum fills utilizing a variety of licks.

In fact, overall, Copeland's drumming is outstanding on this cut, but it was later revealed that parts of six different drum takes were spliced in to create the whole. Stewart later felt it was the wrong approach, telling *Songfacts*: 'I just overdid it. Where was Andy (Summers) when we needed him, because usually, it was Andy who was the limiter of our indulgence. He must have stepped out of the studio'.

The band members knew how special this one was and still do all these years later. Sting said:

I think the lyrics are subtle and well-crafted enough to hit people on a different level from something you just sing along to. It's quite a cleverly put together metaphor. It develops and has an artistic shape to it.

In his book *Lyrics by Sting*, we read the man who wrote it explain as such:

I was pleased that I'd managed a narrative song with a beginning, a middle, and some kind of philosophical resolution in the final verse. If I'd been a more sophisticated songwriter, I would have probably illuminated this change of mood by modulating the third verse into a different key. But it worked anyway.

Every bit of this song is wonderfully conceived and the music is stellar. 'Message in a Bottle' was the album's lead single on 21 September 1979 and was an immediate lightning bolt, topping the UK singles charts for three weeks and also reaching the top spot in Ireland and Spain whilst making the top five in Australia, The Netherlands (where it hit number two), Belgium, France, Canada (where it also hit the number two position) and South Africa. The single also went gold in the UK. Curiously, it struggled in the US, only peaking at number 74 on the *Billboard* Hot 100 despite constant FM airplay. The single did reach number 62 in the US on the Cash Box charts, but even that was surprisingly low considering the legendary status this song has.

Sting owns a winery in Italy that has produced a wine called *Message in a Bottle* (I'm unaware if there really is a message in each bottle, but wouldn't that be nice?). There are well over 100 covers of the song, and Sting played it himself at *Live Aid*.

As for Andy Summers, he summed it up best in his book *One Train Later* by saying: 'For me, it's still the best song Sting ever came up with and the best Police track'.

'Reggatta De Blanc' (Copeland/Sting/Summers)

Technically an instrumental, the title track to the band's album is as vibrant as any song in the catalogue of The Police. As mentioned earlier, this piece originated as a jam during live performances of 'Can't Stand Losing You'. The song was developed further for inclusion on the album to serve as an expansion of the overall running time of *Reggatta de Blanc* and came in at a little over three minutes.

Summers plays some really choice parts and adds harmonics and chiming figures, while Copeland brings in all kinds of dynamics on hi-hat, ride cymbal and snare. Sting adds his mobile bass lines and we get the first true set of his now-infamous 'eeyo' chants, which are so infectious and became a staple of any Police gig.

Despite the chants, The song won the band a Grammy award in 1981 (two years after the initial release) for Best Rock Instrumental Performance.

In 2000, Sting told *Revolver* magazine that:

On the first tour, we had a very short set – only about ten numbers. The songs only lasted two minutes each. And when Stewart was on form, they'd last even less time. So we had about a nine-minute set, right? People would tend to want their money back after that. So we had to extend the songs ad nauseam so we could get paid at the end of the night. Eventually, all the songs began to develop a free-form jazz aspect to them, and that growing sophistication was reflected on the album.

'It's Alright For You' (Copeland/Sting)

A lively song, with some conventional rock moves and some nods to the punk and pop stylings of the earliest days of the band. The song careens along at a catchy pace.

'It's Alright for You' originated from a Stewart Copeland demo on which he played the guitars and drums (and possibly the bass as well). It seems that the rhythm guitars from the demo were kept for this recording and possibly some of the drums. Summers lays down a crackling slide solo for the second and last time with The Police (the other being 'Next to You') and Sting adds some bite and attitude to his vocals, again nodding to punk rock.

'Bring On The Night' (Sting)

A heavy reggae influence underscores this track, which has a mysterious feel to it, with dark verses but light choruses. This is another of the songs that originated during Sting's time in Last Exit and a portion of the lyrics were taken from a song of theirs titled 'Carrion Prince (O Ye of Little Hope)'. The title is taken from a poem about Pontius Pilate by Ted Hughes called *King of Carrion*. Sting didn't stop there with literary references however, he lifted a line from a T.S Eliot poem, *The Love Song of J. Alfred Prufrock* and in his book *Lyrics by Sting,* he was quoted as saying: 'What is it Eliot said? Bad poets borrow, good poets steal?' Even when Sting is being humorous, he still has a great knack for utilizing intelligent references and verbiage. In addition, there are some lyrics that were inspired by Norman Mailer's 1979 Pulitzer Prize-winning book *The Executioner's Song*, so there are lots of references to take in from a song that seems so innocuous. This song is not simply about the night.

Musically, Sting's bass lines are seductive and Summers and Copeland are on top of their game with lots of inventive bits that fill in the spaces. Andy also plays a scorching lead solo and uses some excellent vibrato that adds an edge to the proceedings. The opening of the song is well done, with flanged guitars and then it becomes somewhat jazzy before the obvious reggae of the chorus. Summers plays some lovely arpeggios and shows his versatility throughout without ever doing any guitar heroics. Summers told *Guitar Player Magazine*:

> When I use my fingers I play more with the flesh of the fingers than the nails. It's much more a rhythmic thing than classical guitar style. There is one number, 'Bring on the Night', which is all classical arpeggios up and down the fingerboard, through a flanger. When you're playing it at 2,000 watts through the PA it sounds great.

Stevie Nicks also acknowledged that her first solo hit, the 1981 classic 'Edge of Seventeen' was inspired by this song, which both her guitarist Waddy Wachtel and Andy Summers have also verified. One listen to that chugging intro of the Nicks tune and it's quite obvious, and it worked very well for Stevie and her excellent US hit single. Sting would title his concert documentary film of 1986 after this song and performed a very different version of the track.

Issued as a single in the US, 'Bring on the Night' received some FM airplay. The song did reach the top ten in France, but did not chart in the US and Germany, which were the only other countries where it was released as a single.

'Deathwish' (Copeland/Sting/Summers)

Here's another rocker with all kinds of tempo changes, choppy guitar work and palm-muting. The song is instrumental for nearly the first minute and could have worked in that way, but the morbid lyrics do add a nice juxtaposition to the music. As a kind of wraparound, the song is instrumental for the last minute of the song as well (just like the first minute), simply fading and not exploding into energy one more time like it feels like it should.

As always, Sting is on top of his game on vocals and thumping bass (some of which sounds like it could be from 'Can't Stand Losing You') and the song races at a high speed on the breaks; Stewart adds inventive embellishments with rim shots and bass drum. You can even hear elements of ska in this song, as there's a mix of several styles. The fade works nicely in context.

Andy has some frantic guitar lines, including some rhythmic segments with harmonics in the chorus (which really isn't a chorus, but more of an instrumental break) and instrumental lead in. Summers also uses some really neat delay and choral effects throughout the song.

The lyrics seem to be about suicide, depression or a combination of both. These are subjects explored previously by the band and here it works combined with the riveting music.

In concert, the song was sped up a bit more and used some different chords as well as pedal synthesizers, but the song was eventually dropped from the setlist.

'Walking On The Moon' (Sting)

Many a Police fan's absolute favourite song, 'Walking on the Moon' is without a doubt one of the finest compositions from the pen of Sting.

Inspiration came from the consumption of a few bottles of wine in Munich, Germany where the band were staying. In the 1981 book on the Police by Phil Sutcliffe and Hugh Fielder titled *L'Historia Bandido*, Sting was quoted as saying:

> I was drunk in a hotel room in Munich, slumped on the bed with the whirling pit when this riff came into my head. I got up and starting walking 'round the room singing: 'Walking 'round the room, walking 'round the room'. That was all. In the cool light of morning, I remembered what had happened and I wrote the riff down. But 'Walking 'Round the Room' was a stupid title so I thought of something even more stupid which was 'Walking on the Moon'.

Ah, but let's thank Sting for this 'stupid' title because it couldn't be any better. Andy plays two sparse guitar parts here, leaving a lot of space The reggae undercurrent from the rhythm section of Sting and Stewart allows Sting to go into that signature vocal style. The song is driven largely by Sting's basslines (played on what sounds like a fretless bass) and the drum accents throughout by Stewart are a perfect example of his percussive brilliance. The rim shots and hi-hat work are exemplary and at the 3:15 mark, he provides an amazing clinic on a rare hi-hat solo and for the lengthy outro of the song, he utilizes tricky bass drum pedal patterns. Bubbling underneath all of this is a Roland GR500 guitar synthesizer, adding those spacy sounds that percolate and make the song even more 'moon-like' if you will. Sting adds some 'ey-yo-ey-yo-yo-yo's' during the fade and his personality is all over this track.

Sting added another tale of the inspiration for 'Walking on the Moon' in his memoir *Broken Music*: 'Deborah Anderson was my first real girlfriend ... walking back from Deborah's house in those early days would eventually become a song, for being in love is to be relieved of gravity'. That is actually a very lovely sentiment, isn't it? A very intriguing writing style to note here is how, in each set of verses, Sting sings one line of lyrics and follows up each line with the 'walking on the moon' refrain. This occurs in each verse, each time.

Released on 4 November 1979, 'Walking on the Moon' walked all the way to number one in the UK, making it back-to-back chart toppers from the album for the band. The single was also certified gold. Though the song was not issued as a single in the US, it received and still receives heavy FM airplay. The song would also hit the number one slot in Ireland and the number two position in Italy as well as the top ten in France, Australia and The Netherlands among other territories.

A music video was filmed at the Kennedy Space Center on Merritt Island, FL and has the guys (all in sunglasses) miming to the song with Sting on bass (actually playing the bass notes on guitar), Andy on guitar and Stewart on... the Saturn V moon rocket! Why set up drums when you can play a giant spacecraft? Later shots mix in stock footage and the guys have removed their sunglasses. The video isn't much to speak of and was never aired on MTV, but it provides some laughs. It was much more seen on UK television, due to the song's hit status

'On Any Other Day' (Copeland)

Stewart's songs always added a warped sense of humor, and that is certainly the case here with such couplets describing the nightmare that comes when problems pile on adding to the drudgery of everyday life as in this chorus:

My wife has burned the scrambled eggs
The dog just bit my leg
My teenage daughter ran away
My fine young son has turned out gay
And it would be okay on any other day
And it would be okay on any other day

Vocals are shared between Stewart and Sting and the overall feel is definitely a sarcastic one, with plenty of power chords, mixing in some elements of hard rock, new wave and pop rock. This song is definitely an acquired taste and is one of a few cuts on the album which sound more like B-side material, but it slots in rather nicely. To call this song quirky would be accurate and it does provide levity while rocking along at a nice pace. The deadpan delivery and sarcasm ooze all over the song and it's vintage Stewart.

'The Bed's Too Big Without You' (Sting)

The glorious intro fades in with an insistent reggae groove based around Sting's moving bassline and Stewart's impeccable accents while Andy adds his creative chord sequences. Easily one of the best numbers on the album, the title alone is pure genius and a stark sentiment.

The lyrics are quite harrowing as this song was inspired by a tragedy Sting experienced in which his first girlfriend committed suicide after their breakup and he was understandably moved and upset by this news. Obviously, there is darkness in this song, but it can also be seen as a sincere lament and contemplation.

There are musical gaps at times, with just drums and bass that add to the feel and despite the fact that the song really doesn't have any musical changes, it still works very well. The arrangement is effective in that the title is sung the first two times through on the chorus, but the third and last time, there is a gap before the 'without you' part that changes things up, showing an uncanny sense of dynamics and how to use them to good effect.

An alternate version of this song was recorded in mono and first appeared on the *Six Pack* singles box in the UK in 1980 and was later included on the box set *Message in a Box: The Complete Recordings* in 1993. This was another song resurrected from Sting's days in Last Exit.

'Contact' (Copeland)

Another song from the warped mind of Stewart Copeland that is as strange as you'd expect, but also has an odd appeal. The throbbing bass and angular guitars are prominent in the mix and Sting somehow sings lyrics such as: 'I've got a lump in my throat about the note you wrote, I'd come on over, but I haven't got a raincoat' with enough conviction to pull it off.

Complete in just over two and a half minutes, 'Contact' is somewhat filler material, but it is still effective enough to merit inclusion on the album and really, anytime Stewart is writing a song, you know you're in for something unusual, twisted, a shade bizarre and always interesting.

This track is one that works well within the context of new wave and what would later be described as alternative rock. There's no question that Stewart wrote the weird, quirky, offbeat material and that by album three, Sting seemed to have had his fill of that.

And the songs Stewart wrote for The Police from *Zenyatta Mondatta* onward did take on a more accessible style and sound that showed he could really come up with some intricate material. That's what makes his writing on *Reggatta de Blanc* with songs like 'Contact' such a fun listen because songs like these wouldn't find their way onto The Police albums again.

'Does Everyone Stare' (Copeland)

Starting off with jazz inflected bass and off-kilter piano, with a dash of spoken word (by Stewart), we are once again taken into Copeland's demented genius. The song is actually quite catchy in the chorus and Sting sings perfectly to match the song's whimsical nature whilst also adding a pulsating bassline.

At the beginning of the track, we faintly hear some opera singing, which actually leaked through the tape machine as Stewart was recording the piano part in his home for the demo and decided to leave it in, though it was actually Andy who played the piano part in the studio.

The lyrics truly nail the idea of insecurity:

I'm gonna write you a sonnet but I don't know where to start
I'm so used to laughing at the things in my heart

Last of all I'm sorry 'cos you never asked for this
I can see I'm not your type and my shot will always miss.

Ouch!

'No Time This Time' (Sting)

Oddly, this song had already been featured as a B-side to the 'So Lonely'
single in 1979 and had been recorded during the sessions for the debut
album in 1978. It had gone down well live and thus, the band went with it to
end *Reggatta de Blanc*.

If there's any doubt as to why Stewart Copeland is one of the greatest
drummers in the world, then just listen to the zany, frenetic drumming
throughout this breakneck track, which cruises at Mach speed. The drum
intro is crazed enough and it doesn't let up from there. Let's not forget the
speedy bass and guitar playing that snakes in underneath and piles on the
madness.

Sting's vocals are also high up in the stratosphere and when Summers
lays on the power chords for the chorus, Sting kicks it up another notch.
Andy also has a biting guitar solo and the song eventually winds down with
some Sting vocal refrains and the band pulling a few stop/starts, allowing
Copeland to fill in the spaces with drum fills. Sadly, his best fill is just at the
very end of the fade and hard to hear, but no doubt about it – this tune is
terrific and throws punk, new wave and hard rock into a melting pot at an
exhilarating speed.

Reggatta De Blanc Rarities
'Visions Of The Night' (Sting)

This four-on-the-floor rocker was actually from the 1977 sessions with John
Cale but wasn't released until it was used as a B-side for the 'Walking on the
Moon' single in 1979. Sting, It was one of the numbers they did during the
Strontum 90 demo sessions.

That version (more on it later) isn't a whole lot different from what ended
up being recorded by The Police with John Cale. Sting really channels his
energy vocally and Summers provides hard rocking chords, melodic lead
lines and a great intro riff. Henry Padovani is also on there supposedly, as his
rhythm guitar was apparently kept and added on to (which is odd since he
had struggled with rhythm playing in the studio), so that makes this the only
time all four Police members are on a song – if indeed that is accurate. This
is a combination of two different takes, – one with Henry and one with Andy.
The 1978 recording of the song remains unreleased.

In the notes on the 1993 *Message in a Box: The Complete Recordings* box
set, Sting states: 'That was the first song I wrote after going to London. It was
hard to be serious about the whole thing. I was bemused, much to Stewart's
disgust'. Andy also commented on this song in the box set and said: 'It was

one of the first things Sting played me and I thought, Christ, this is a number one! Which it wasn't, of course, but I was taken with the spark of it'. Stewart chimed in: 'The title was too cerebral for our early audiences, so Sting would announce it as 'Three O'Clock Shit'.

'Three O'Clock Shit' would also be recorded by Strontium 90 as 'Three O'Clock Shot' and one can hear the main guitar riff of 'Be My Girl-Sally' and some lyrics that would later be used in 1983 for 'O My God'. In any case, this convoluted history of 'Visions of the Night' aside, the song is a great Police punk rocker and it was also part of the live set for several years.

Zenyatta Mondatta (1980)

Personnel:
Sting: bass, lead vocals, backing vocals, synthesizer
Andy Summers: guitars, backing vocals, piano, synthesizer and bass on 'Behind My Camel'
Stewart Copeland: drums, percussion, backing vocals
Released: 3 October 1980
Recorded: Wisseloord Studios (Hilversum, The Netherlands)
Produced by: The Police and Nigel Gray
Engineer: Nigel Gray
Cover Design: Michael Ross
Highest chart position: UK: 1, US: 5, Canada: 2, Japan: 16, Germany: 5, Australia: 1

The Police went all around the world to support the *Reggatta de Blanc* album. In March 1980, they began an epic jaunt, which took them to quite a few locales that were highly unusual for rock bands to perform at. Stops included Egypt, Taiwan, Greece, India, Hong Kong and Mexico. It was an ambitious strategy of Miles Copeland, but it exhausted the band beyond belief. A documentary of this amazing tour was captured on film and released in 1982 with the apt title *The Police Around the World*. It featured a mixture of concert footage and the insanity behind the scenes. It was directed by Kate and Derek Burbidge – Derek had done the band's music videos prior to this and they had a very good working relationship.

The band did not have much time to write, and were unable to record in the UK because of the strict tax laws, so they booked a studio in The Netherlands that had a lot of excellent clients in the past, named Wisseloord Studios in Hilversum. Among the legends that have recorded there are Elton John, Tina Turner, Def Leppard, Genesis, Golden Earring, U2, and The Stranglers.

Once again, Nigel Gray would co-produce and engineer. The album was recorded in only three weeks and then it was right back on the road with no time to spare. In fact, in *L'Historia Bandito*, Copeland was quoted as saying:

> We had bitten off more than we could chew ... we finished the album at 4 am on the day we were starting our next world tour. We went to bed for a few hours and then travelled down to Belgium for the first gig. It was cutting it very fine.

It's no exaggeration – The Police completed the album at 4 am and then played a gig in Werchter, Belgium at 9 pm that same night.

Although *Zenyatta Mondatta* confirmed the band as international superstars and sold in huge quantities, the band were actually unhappy with the outcome. They had had very little time to write and rehearse and as a result, there were two instrumentals and a few rather short songs. This album was also where Sting really started getting more verbose and using a lot of literary references (as well as writing nearly all the material) and the production and mixing were top-notch, all the more amazing, given that the timeframe was so condensed. Although the album is a tad patchy and far from a perfect, there is still so much good material. That being said, for the record to have come out as good as it did is pretty remarkable.

Copeland told *Mojo*: 'Zenyatta was the cusp between the thrill of conquering the world and the responsibility of being the conqueror'. He also told Phil Sutcliffe in the feature:

Big record company honchos would hang out in the studio, discussing sales figures and pulling Sting aside. We were acutely aware that we were creating a product for the marketplace. The relationship between ourselves got pretty heated under those condensed conditions.

As for the album title, Copeland offered up this explanation to writer Chris Welch:

It means everything. It's the same explanation that applies to the last two (albums). It doesn't have a specific meaning like 'Police Brutality' or 'Police Arrest', or anything predictable like that. Being vague, it says a lot more. You can interpret it in a lot of different ways. It's not an attempt to be mysterious, just syllables that sound good together, like the sound of a melody that has no words at all, has a meaning.

Both words in the title are made up, but it worked and rolled off the tongue rather well.

Zenyatta Mondatta was to be a massive hit for The Police when released on 3 October 1980 and it was to be their second number one album in the UK, as well as their first album to reach the US top ten, where it peaked at number five. Sales in the US were double platinum and platinum in the UK, Canada, Australia and many other territories. The album effectively spent three straight years on the US charts, being there for a total of 153 weeks. Two singles would grace the top ten in both the US and the UK as well. The 1980-81 tour sold out everywhere The Police performed and it was quite obvious that from this point on Sting would be dominating the proceedings in the writing department.

The tour was the longest yet for the band and began on 26 July 1980 at the Milton Keynes Bowl in the UK and concluded in Australia on 26 February 1981. Attendance was at an all-time high and The Police were now looked at as a major act. Their time had arrived.

The late Jerry Moss (he was the 'M' as part of the A&M Records team) and his wife Ann owned a racehorse and named her Zenyatta after the Police album. The horse would finish her career winning nineteen out of twenty races and is now in the *National Museum Of Racing And Hall Of Fame*. Sting was on hand to see her win the 2009 *Breeder's Cup Classic*. So it turns out, Zenyatta proved to be quite a successful made-up name.

'Don't Stand So Close To Me' (Sting)

Here, we have one of Sting's masterpieces and a truly legendary song. Opening rather ominously with a brooding synthesizer and a few muted guitar notes, it almost sounds as if the band is warming up. When Stewart comes in with his hi-hat and pulsating bass drum, the feel changes, but the tone is still dark with minor chords at the fore.

Sting's lyrics tell this forbidden tale of student and teacher. The female student has feelings of desire for her teacher, who feels frustration and guilt at being unable to act on his impulses, but also knowing he must refrain from action. An inspiration is the famous novel *Lolita* by Vladimir Nabokov and Sting somehow manages to get Nabokov's surname in the lyrics, while rhyming it with the word 'cough'.

The band's mastery of dynamics is on full display here as the second set of verses now use upbeat drumming, which changes the feel, and the chorus is so infectious you almost forget the subject. Throughout, Stewart's drumming is impeccable as always, especially his use of ride cymbal whilst the mid-section features some chord washes played on guitar synthesizer.

While there's still an undercurrent of reggae here, it's not as pronounced as past singles. The song proved to be a monster hit when released as a single on 19 September 1980, topping the UK singles charts for four weeks and achieving gold status, while it would reach number ten in the US in April 1981 and charted a total of 18 weeks. The single would also top the charts in Ireland and Spain, soared to number two in Canada and New Zealand and number three in Italy, The Netherlands, South Africa and Australia.

The music video was the first with any kind of concept, featuring the guys in a classroom with Sting as teacher, Stewart playing air drums and Andy miming on guitar. A female student tries to get close to Sting, but of course, she's not allowed to 'stand so close' to him! This video was played heavily on MTV once the channel took to the airwaves in summer 1981 and the song would win a Grammy award for Best Rock Performance by a Duo or Group with Vocal in 1982. In 1980 it was also the best-selling single of the year in the UK.

'Don't Stand So Close to Me' would live several lives in the 1980s and one such instance was in 1985 when Sting made a guest appearance on what would become a worldwide sensation for Dire Straits: 'Money for Nothing'. Sting did backing vocals on the song and also sang the now-infamous 'I want my MTV' line over the intro amongst a barrage of moody keyboards, which led to a brief drum solo before those familiar power chords of the song kicked in. It was eventually noticed that the way Sting sang the 'I want my MTV' line was using the exact same melody line as 'Don't Stand So Close to Me'.

What had happened was that Dire Straits were recording their *Brothers in Arms* album in Montserrat and Sting was nearby as he liked to windsurf there. Sting heard the playback of the track and according to Dire Straits bassist John Illsley and said, 'You've done it this time, you bastards'. He knew how good it was.

According to Illsley in an interview with *Classic Rock Magazine*: 'Mark (Knopfler) said if he thought it was so good, why didn't he (Sting) go and add something to it. He did his bit there and then'. Sting would join Dire Straits on stage at the *Live Aid* concert to perform the song in rousing fashion on 13 July 1985 at Wembley Stadium.

Sting would receive a co-writing credit but stated that he felt embarrassed by it. As he later stated, he did indeed get money for nothing.

The song would also be reworked in 1986 in a new arrangement as 'Don't Stand So Close to Me '86' and became a hit all over again, although nowhere near as big as the original version. More on this recording later.

'Driven To Tears' (Sting)

Here was the first truly political song from Sting with lyrics that are as pertinent now as they were in 1980. The inspiration for the song goes back to when The Police were touring the US for *Reggatta de Blanc* and Sting saw a report on starving children in Biafra on television while sitting in his hotel room. Horrified by the images he saw, Sting stated that the title came to him as he was literally driven to tears watching the report.

This theme and song would go a long way towards influencing awareness about the impoverished nations with starving people (which most of the world was oblivious to) that led to the creation of Band Aid in 1984 and the song 'Do They Know It's Christmas?', plus the *Live Aid* concerts of 1985, which Sting supported.

All three players are at the top of their game and Andy Summers has a nasty, tension-filled guitar solo that stands as one of his very best. Andy's chiming chords also add to the palette of colours on the spectrum.

Stewart's drumming includes a dazzling display of hi-hat, other cymbals and lots of fills in the brief spaces between Sting's lyrics. Sting punctuates with his bass and his vocals had by this point, achieved a new maturity and sophistication that the first two albums didn't quite reach. His signature vocal refrains of 'woh, oh, oh' in the bridge leading to the guitar solo were built for the live stage.

The lyrics pull no punches. The message is a commentary on the divide between the rich and the poor; the haves and the have-nots.

Sting played this at *Live Aid* in 1985 in a sparse arrangement in which he quietly strummed electric guitar with Branford Marsalis providing poignant saxophone. The Police also played this at each of the three shows they did in 1986 on the *Conspiracy of Hope Tour* for Amnesty International. The song has been covered a few times, most notably by Pearl Jam at some live shows and actor Robert Downey Jr., who sang a blistering version with Sting and his band at Sting's 60th birthday celebration that brought down the house.

While 'Driven to Tears' was not issued as a single, it received considerable US radio play and peaked at number 35 on the album rock charts in 1981.

'When The World Is Running Down, You Make the Best Of What's Still Around' (Sting)

Sometimes simplicity can work wonders and such is the case with this track, which has the distinct honour of being the Police song with the longest title.

This track's groove is tight; the insistent beat and those three chiming chords on guitar are buoyed by fat bass grooves and Sting's vocals that accent the song and melody. The only real change in the song is when, about two minutes in, a new bass/drum groove hits and Andy Summers plays a one-note solo that slowly rises before the return of the main groove.

The lyrics are also excellent and Sting just rattles them off in a personable way that makes it sound as if he's telling the listener exactly what's going on in his mind.

Mentioned in the lyris, the *T.A.M.I. Show* was the name of a concert documentary film from 1964 shot in Santa Monica, CA, that featured an awesome mix of acts playing live, including The Rolling Stones, Beach Boys, Chuck Berry, Marvin Gaye, James Brown, The Supremes and more. T.A.M.I stood for *Teenage Awards Music International* or *Teen Age Music International,* depending on what the producers of the show decided. In any case, it's an obvious reference by Sting to this awesome concert film, which featured some of his big influences. In a radio interview in Baltimore, MD, with King Crimson leader Robert Fripp, Summers recalled:

I thought that the lyrics were great that Sting had. Nothing like what we finally came up with. It was like this sort of disco song with different chords and everything. I know there was quite some friction in the studio over that particular piece. And we worked through it and we finally came up with it. Without bragging, overly, if I had not put those chords on and put the guitar sound that is so characteristic, it wouldn't have sounded anything like it does now.

Though the song was not a single, it was played constantly on US rock radio and became a huge fan favorite. This tune also proved to be a winner in concert and the performances on the 2007-08 reunion tour were excellent and involved improved jamming.

Twenty years later, in 2000, a remix was done of this song by DJs Gino Scaletti and Quinn Whalley as Different Gear. It became a hit in clubs and A&M Records got wind of it; the label decided to issue it as a single credited to Different Gear versus The Police and consequently, it hit number seven on the US Dance charts (under the title 'When the World is Runnin' Down (You Can't Go Wrong)' and the top 30 on the UK singles charts.

'Canary In A Coalmine' (Sting)
Deliriously punchy and funky, 'Canary in a Coalmine' is a bouncy track that is over in less than two and a half minutes. The song actually originated while the band were touring Japan in 1980 and Sting recorded a solo demo of it later that summer. The finished version wasn't too dissimilar from Sting's demo, but Andy and Stewart really made it come to life.

Andy's choppy, funky guitar riffs are as infectious as Sting's melody line. Stewart plays an irresistible groove and Sting's multi-tracked harmony vocals are also a key element.

There's only one brief letup in the pace and rhythm provided by Andy's tinkling piano. Toots & The Maytals would cover this song a number of years later on a Police tribute album called *Reggatta de Mondatta Volume II*.

'Voices Inside My Head' (Sting)
Beginning with an delectable groove, this song is not too dissimilar from 'Reggatta de Blanc' in that it is largely instrumental but does have some vocal parts and chants. There are some sparse lyrics that repeat, but they're really just there for melody.

The bass playing has Sting embossed in a fat lick that is accompanied by choral guitar parts that repeat from Andy and tight drumming by Stewart. In the mid-section, it changes to some scratch guitar while Copeland throws down some exquisite solos. The insistent melody gets right in the listener's head and there is a joyous feel once Sting comes in with his vocals. This track was played over the PA system before their 1980-81 shows using a different mix.

Paired with 'When the World is Running Down, You Make the Best of What's Still Around' for club play, this mix would rise to number three on the US dance charts beginning in November 1980 and charted for a whopping 21 weeks.

On the reunion tour of 2007-08, they played it in a different key and arrangement that was much slower-paced and used some guitar synth sounds before merging into 'When the World is Running Down...' as a medley, the pace kicking up from that point forward. Andy let loose with an extensive, wailing three-minute guitar solo while Sting laid down some crazy jazz-inflected bass fills and Stewart pounded away. This was one of the highlights of the set.

'Bombs Away' (Copeland)
Stewart Copeland wrote this one and his drumming is outstanding, while Sting's snaky basslines weave in and out a suitable bedrock beneath Andy's mix of clean notes and harmonics, not to mention a blazing solo that almost seems to come out of nowhere.

Perhaps Stewart's experiences growing up and moving all over the world, being the son of a C.I.A. agent, inspired some of these lyrics. This is a rare move into more topical and political territory for Copeland, although the catchy chorus and goofy line, 'Bombs away, in old Bombay' might exist solely for rhyming reasons. The song was inspired by the recent invasion of Afghanistan by the Soviet Union. And there's no question Stewart is venting his anger, shown here in the opening verses:

> The general scratches his belly and thinks
> His pay is good but his officers stink
> Guerilla girl, hard and sweet
> A military man would love to meet
> The President looks in the mirror and speaks
> His shirts are clean but his country reeks

As for the music, Copeland told writer Chris Welch:

> 'Bombs Away' was written on a Siouxsie and the Banshees backing track. I changed the speed and did things to the EQ to change the drum pattern. So with the desk, I can get my song playing, then press a switch, and there's Siouxsie singing away.

'De Do Do Do, De Da Da Da' (Sting)
Sting really hit it upon the head with this song. One of the main reasons Sting utilized such a silly, almost childlike title was because he had stated that he felt too often people were paying little attention to the lyrical content in songs and were more focused on the beat, rhythm and melodic parts.

In this instance, the lyrics still remain sophisticated, but the song might have proved Sting's point, because how many people really honed in on the lyrics aside from the chorus? Sting was even quoted as saying, 'The lyrics are about banality, about the abuse of words...the lyrics have an internal logic'. In an interview with *Rolling Stone* in 1988, Sting commented further:

> I was trying to make an intellectual point about how the simple can be so powerful. Why are our favourite songs 'Da Doo Ron Ron' and 'Do Wah Diddy Diddy'? In the song, I tried to address that issue. But everyone said, 'This is bullshit, child's play'. No one listened to the lyrics. Listen to the lyrics.

I'll say it again and again, but The Police were masters at arranging songs, finding accented nuances, using open spaces properly and executing dynamics. It's all on display in this song. Andy Summers plays effective muted chords on the verses and then lively chords that jangle and change the mood in the pre-chorus and chorus. Sting and Stewart stay in the pocket rhythmically and play for the song, not against it, with too much interplay. The way the song ends with those muted chords that lead to the fade out is very unusual..

Issued as the first single from the album in the US and the second single from the album in the UK on 5 December 1980, the song became a top ten winner on both sides of the Atlantic, peaking at number ten in America and number five in Britain where it would chart for eight weeks and went gold. The song would also reach number two in Canada, Ireland and Spain and made the top ten in Australia, France, New Zealand and South Africa, proving to be a solid hit in Germany and The Netherlands as well.

Sting recorded this as a solo demo in the summer of 1980 and then the band were presented it and worked out all the arrangements. Later on, in December of 1980, Sting was in Miami, where producer Nigel Gray happened to be, as he was producing the Wishbone Ash album *Number the Brave*. They booked some studio time and knocked out both Spanish and Japanese language versions, which were both issued as singles. These were mixed just before Christmas on 14 December 1980. Sadly, neither of these recordings have surfaced on a Police compilation or box set. They are also mixed differently with bass being more prominent and the drums mixed dry and lower in the mix. In fact, it sounds like Sting may have even re-recorded the bass parts. No word as to whether Sting wanted to do versions in Icelandic, Russian or Klingon, but it was probably on the table.

In 1986, The Police gave this a go for the purported new studio album of re-recordings that ended up as the greatest hits package, *Every Breath You Take: The Singles*. It remained unreleased until it was included only on the DTS and SACD versions of the 2003 release *Every Breath You Take: The Classics*. More on this later on …

'Behind My Camel' (Summers)

The story on this song is legend, and it's hysterical. Only in The Police could you have such hatred for a song amongst the band members and have it lead to utterly ridiculous results.

Sting and Stewart were not fans of this song, and in fact, Sting loathed it. As such, Sting refused to play bass on it. Producer Nigel Gray was quoted in the Chris Campion book *Walking on the Moon* as to how the title came about: 'He (Summers) didn't tell me this himself, but I'm 98% sure the reason is this: what would you find behind a camel? A monumental pile of shit'.

Sting would definitely agree. In the magazine *Revolver*, Sting told the interviewer:

I hated that song so much that, one day, when I was in the studio, I found the tape lying on the table. So I took it around the back of the studio and actually buried it in the garden.

Whether that's truth or an embellishment, it doesn't matter because it's hilarious and it definitely proves he hadn't changed his stance on the song, even twenty years later.

As for Stewart's point of view, in the same magazine article, he said:

> As hard done by as I ever felt in this band, I could always take comfort in the fact that Andy got shafted even worse than I did on that little instrumental. Sting didn't even bother to play on it. Andy played all the bass and guitars, and I only played on the song because there wasn't anyone else to play drums.

So, is it that bad of a song? No. It is quite weird and eerie, it has a distinct Middle-Eastern flavour and it feels like someone played 'Kashmir' from Led Zeppelin on a warped cassette that sat in the sun for a few months. Summers' personality is all over this track and he plays all the instruments except drums.

Andy had the last laugh when this somehow won a Grammy award for Best Rock Instrumental Performance in 1982. 'Behind My Camel' beat out 'YYZ' by Rush, 'Computer World' by Kraftwerk, 'Unsung Heroes' by the Dixie Dregs and Robert Fripp's 'The League of Gentlemen' (that last one being especially ironic as Summers and Fripp would do a successful album together later that year).

The awesome alternative-rock trio Primus would cover 'Behind My Camel' on their 1998 mini-LP *Rhinoplasty*. On the Primus website, Les Claypool stated why the band covered this oddity:

> I've always wanted to cover a Police song. We've jammed on several of their tunes, but Sting's vocal parts are, to say the least, a bit too challenging for me. An instrumental seemed the logical option to choose. Brain (drummer Brian 'Brain' Mantia) plays exceptionally well on this tune.

Obviously impressed and flattered, Copeland befriended Les and ended up producing the song 'Dirty Drowning Man' on the 1999 Primus album *Antipop* and a few years later, Claypool would be in the band Oysterhead with Stewart and Trey Anastasio.

'Man In A Suitcase' (Sting)

An upbeat, sunny song with a distinct reggae flavour and a beat you can dance to, this song had the distinguished honour of coming after 'Behind My Camel' on the album's second side of vinyl. 'Man in a Suitcase' is instantly hummable and punchy. While many (including me) felt this was about the tediousness of life on the road and going from hotel to hotel, apparently, it was inspired by a British TV spy series.

Sting's basslines are consistently moving through the song and play a key element in the groove. The way Copeland switches from hi-hat to ride cymbal from verse to chorus is almost like adding another instrument – the knowledge of dynamics is ingenious.

The mid-section is just a few notes on guitar accompanied by what sounds like audio in an airport (this is also on the intro), and then the key changes for the rest of the song. Sting's voice is layered, on the infectious choruses, which make the song all the more free-spirited. Over in just 2:19, it's surprising this one wasn't tried as a single, but no matter – the fans loved it anyway.

An excellent live version was used as a B-side on a double single of 'Every Breath You Take' in the UK in 1983 and was included on the 1993 box set.

'Shadows In The Rain' (Sting)
If you want an example of perfect synchronicity (yes, I said it) between three musicians, look no further than this jewel. Sting and Stewart are so locked in, so tight, so connected to the groove they've created that it's an honour and a pleasure to hear.

This was another that Sting demoed on his own in Ireland in the summer of 1980 and that arrangement is much closer to the way he would rework it for his debut solo album, *The Dream of the Blue Turtles,* in 1985 (more on that in the Sting section).

After a brief cymbal lead-in, the ultra-fat bass groove and snap-tight snare drum are nothing short of intoxicating. There's also a crispness to each accent from the drums that is an example of how good Nigel Gray was with his mixing. The snare drum sound on this track is sublime.Andy isn't absent here as he adds some faint squeals and gnarling sounds out of his guitar that seem inspired by his pal Robert Fripp.

'The Other Way Of Stopping' (Copeland)
An instrumental, this song features example after example of Stewart Copeland's excellence, not just as a drummer but as a percussionist and writer, as this was his composition. The band may have been short on material to have two instrumentals on the album, but with a band as cool as The Police, that's not necessarily a bad thing. Andy's artsy, dissonant guitars and Sting's insistent bass playing are definitely from the school of new wave, and you could hear that bands like Missing Persons, Echo & Bunnymen and Siouxsie and the Banshees knew of The Police.

'The Other Way of Stopping' is definitely a piece of music that points towards Stewart's later soundtrack work for television and cinema, where he achieved an incredible amount of success.

Zenyatta Mondatta Rarities
'Friends' (Summers)
To say the least, this was not in contention for being the theme song of the popular TV sitcom *Friends*, though I wish it was. 'Friends' came from the

demented mind of Andy Summers and couldn't have been anything other than a B-side. Then again, 'Mother' made it to an album …

This warped treatise on cannibalism has Andy in his 'Be My Girl-Sally' accent, discussing his eating habits. It was a novel that inspired Summers to charm us with this ditty, as he explained in the *Message in a Box* liner notes:

I wrote it as a take on *Stranger in a Strange Land*, the Robert Heinlein science fiction novel. It was about eating your friends, or 'grocking' them as the book put it. 'I likes to eat my friends and make no bones about it, I likes to eat my friends, I couldn't do without it'. Very quirky. A touch of Long John Silver on acid.

'Friends' would be used as the B-side to the 'Don't Stand So Close to Me' single and most likely shocked the hell out of casual fans who bought the single. It appears on both box sets.

'A Sermon' (Copeland)
This punk rocker was written by Copeland in 1978 and was called 'No Excuse' for a while before ending up as 'A Sermon'. The song sounds nothing at all like the material on *Zenyatta Mondatta* and that's because it was recorded during the *Outlandos d'Amour* sessions in April 1978 and was left off the album before finally serving a purpose on the B-side for the 'De Do Do Do, De Da Da Da' single.

Lyrically, 'A Sermon' has Copeland railing against the record industry and he has some pithy lines such as the opening: 'When you reach number ten, And think the struggle ends, But it ain't the end, It's only a trend'.

What's especially effective about Stewart's writing for this song is the changing chart placings, which incrementally become higher in each verse: from number ten, to number eight, to number four, and of course, ultimately hitting number one. While this idea was in used in a more sophisticated fashion by Billy Joel on his 1974 US Top 40 hit 'The Entertainer', one must give Stew some credit for venting about the vacuous industry they were now aspiring to be a part of.

In the box set notes in 1993, Sting said:

That's Stewart's song about making it, which was a bit presumptuous because we only just had. It's arrogant, but Stewart is good at being arrogant in a funny way – as in that Klark Kent line about 'If you don't like me, you can suck my socks.

Stewart added:

We hadn't made it at all when we did this song. And we were just as arrogant as each other from the start. At least success never changed us.

Andy let me play most of the guitar, including the intro riff. He did the clever bit in the middle.

This song ended up on the 1993 box set *Message in a Box* and also appears on the *Flexible Strategies* rarities disc for the *Every Move You Make: The Studio Recordings* box in 2019.

Ghost In The Machine (1981)

Personnel:
Sting: bass, lead vocals, backing vocals, keyboards, saxophone
Andy Summers: guitars, backing vocals, keyboards
Stewart Copeland: drums, percussion, keyboards, backing vocals
Additional musicians:
Jean Rousell: keyboards on 'Every Little Thing She Does is Magic'
Released: 2 October 1981
Recorded: AIR Studios (Montserrat), Le Studio (Montreal, Quebec, Canada)
Produced by: The Police and Hugh Padgham
Engineer: Hugh Padgham
Cover Design: Mick Haggerty
Highest chart position: UK: 1, US: 2, Canada: 1, Japan: 29, Germany: 4, Australia: 1

The Police had a hugely successful tour in 1980-81 that catapulted them to superstardom, and almost exactly one year to the day from the release of *Zenyatta Mondatta*, the band issued their fourth album titled *Ghost in the Machine*. Changes were afoot with this album as the band went to two new studios (AIR in Montserrat and Le Studio in Montreal) and also hired the brilliant Hugh Padgham (Phil Collins, XTC, Genesis, Split Enz, Peter Gabriel, Human League) in a quest for new sounds and a new approach.

Sting was taking control at this point and his desire to bring keyboards and saxophones into the mix, to the detriment of the guitars, which did not sit so well with the others. Despite the tension created by this, *Ghost in the Machine* remains the best Police album. From start to finish, the album has an atmosphere that the others could not capture and the new sonic additions really pushed the sound forward, with Hugh Padgham helping to bring all of that to the surface.

In his autobiography, Summers said this about the band and the album:

I have to say, I was getting disappointed with the musical direction around the time of *Ghost in the Machine*. With the horns and synth coming in, the fantastic raw-trio feel – all the really creative and dynamic stuff – was being lost. We were ending up backing a singer doing his pop songs.

A lot of turmoil occurred during the sessions. Stewart and Andy were feeling slighted by Sting and working conditions were deteriorating. Stewart said at the time, 'We're starting not to support each other...it's getting lonely in this band...'

Sting knew what he was doing, however, because this album confirmed that The Police were one of the biggest musical acts in the world. The album topped the charts in the UK, Canada, The Netherlands and Australia, hit number two in the US and went top ten just about everywhere else whilst also going platinum in the UK and triple platinum in the US, with over three million sold. There were four hit singles worldwide and the videos were all over the brand-new MTV, which started up in 1981. The album tallied a whopping 109 weeks on the US album charts.

Ghost in the Machine received universally excellent reviews and accolades upon its release on 2 October 1981 and is still well thought of today. In fact, the album is ranked at number 322 on *Rolling Stone's 500 Greatest Albums of All Time*, number 76 on the *Q Magazine 100 Greatest British Albums Ever*, number 86 on *Pitchfork*'s list of *100 Best Albums of the 1980s* and *The Guardian* had the album in its *1000 Albums to Hear Before You Die* list in 2007.

The album's title came from a novel written by author Arthur Koestler and this made it the first Police album to have an English-language title. As for the album's cover, it also marked a change as it did not feature a photo of the band, but rather a graphic that depicted the heads of the three band members and their distinctive hair styles, beginning with Andy on the left, Sting in the middle and ending with Stewart on the right. The design was by Mick Haggerty, who had done covers for ELO, Supertramp (he would win a Grammy for his design on that band's *Breakfast in America*), Gamma and David Bowie, among others. This album would change the dynamics within The Police from hereon in, but the music did not suffer for it one bit.

The 1981-82 tour for the album was a massive success, with the band filling arenas all around the world, having become one of the biggest acts in the business. The band played 100 shows from 1 October 1981 until 6 September 1982 and most were sellouts.

Showing a reflection of the band's expanding sound, a horn section called The Chops accompanied The Police on the tour and featured Darryl Dixon, David Watson and Marvin Daniels. The decision to use a horn section showed just how much control Sting had at this point as Andy and Stewart didn't feel the need for extra players on the album, let alone the tour, but had no choice but to comply.

'Spirits In The Material World' (Sting)
While this album opener ushered in a new musical era for The Police, it's not like it was such a drastic turn that their sound was compromised. 'Spirits in the Material World' is as ghostly as its title in the way the guitars and keyboards intertwine and add an eerie, chilling atmosphere. The bass bubbles and the drums are more subtle than normal, but Stewart adds all kinds of neat inflections and uses his arsenal with aplomb– his personality remains stamped on this song. There's a ska vibe in the verses and a more straightforward rock form used in the choruses.

It's Andy who seems a little in the background here, but he finds intricate patterns to weave in and out of – he is most definitely not forgotten despite his frustrations. The song has no solo as such, but does feature a few keyboard notes that dance in the middle where one might have been, but it works well despite the simplicity.

Sting said in the band's tour program in 1983:

'Spirits in the Material World' was written on one of those Casio keyboards while I was riding in the back of a truck somewhere. I just tap, tap, tap and there it was, just by accident. That was the first time I'd ever touched a synthesizer, that album.

Sting was so close to the song that he initially didn't even want Andy to play on it and insisted he (Sting) play the parts on synthesizer. Not surprisingly, there were arguments and thankfully, Summers won out, although his guitars are so blended in with the keyboards that they are not very prominent. Andy told *Guitar Player* magazine in 1982 about his playing on the song:

Actually, that is just a guitar played up very high and plucked dry – you know, the palm on the string. I blended this with the setting on the Prophet 5 keyboard synthesizer to get that kind of sound.

The song is one of several that Sting was inspired to write based on the writings of the aforementioned Arthur Koestler, who believed that outside influences could destroy our spirit and restrict our thinking. The spirits and ghosts Koestler alluded to were the innate higher functions that often get lost in the 'machine' created by governments and corporations, which is obviously something Sting tapped into here. Perhaps he was saying that we are all the spirits in this material world, which places such an emphasis on goods, money and fame.

In his book *Lyrics by Sting*, Mr. Sumner explained:

I thought that while political progress is clearly important in resolving conflict around the world, there are spiritual (as opposed to religious) aspects of our recovery that also need to be addressed. I suppose by 'spiritual', I mean the ability to see the bigger picture, to be able to step outside the narrow box of our conditioning and access those higher modes of thinking that Koestler talked about. Without this, politics is just the rhetoric of failure.

The single was a hit, just missing the top ten in both the UK (where it hit number 12), the US (where it peaked at number 11 and charted a total of 13 weeks) and Canada (cresting in at number 13). The single also made the top ten in France, The Netherlands and Ireland. Furthermore, the single sold well enough to go silver in the UK.

The music video featured the band playing the song in the studio, which was dimly lit and all over MTV, having only taken to the airwaves a few months before the album's release. Reaching number seven on US rock radio, the song was also a staple on FM rock stations and became a live favourite, though it was usually played in a different key and sounded a little off without the keyboard parts (though they did utilize some pedal synths). In 1995, Pato Banton covered the song with Sting for the soundtrack of *Ace Ventura: When Nature Calls* and it made the UK top 40 as a single.

'Every Little Thing She Does Is Magic' (Sting)

One of the greatest Police songs, 'Every Little Thing She Does is Magic' began way back in 1976 as a Sting solo demo (this demo would later resurface on the Strontium 90 collection in 1997, which is discussed later on in the book), before it was then revisited in January 1981 when Sting recorded a demo version with keyboardist Jean Roussel (who had played many years with Cat Stevens and had done sessions with acts like Thin Lizzy, 10cc, Joe Cocker, Peter Frampton, Miles Davis, Joan Armatrading and Osibisa among many others). On this demo, the pair of Sting and Roussel played all the instruments and at one point, the track was considered for inclusion on a solo album Sting was thinking about doing.

A few months later, Roussel got a call to come down to AIR Studios in Montserrat and re-record his keyboard parts from the demo because The Police were now recording this song for their upcoming album. This was met with serious resistance from Stewart and in particular, Andy. After about a week, it was deemed that the original demo keyboard could not be bested and thus, the band would record over Roussel's original demo recording heard on the album.

Sting met so much resistance on this song throughout the recording – it's truly amazing the song got completed at all. He told *The Independent* in 1993:

> This was first recorded as a demo, with the piano figure, in a studio in Montreal. I had written the song long before the Police were successful, but it seemed a bit soft for the band at first. But the demo was really great. It sounded like a number one song to me. I took it to the band, who were reticent, still thinking it was soft. I was saying, 'But listen, it's a hit'. We tried to do it from scratch as The Police, but it didn't have the same energy as the demo. After a degree of hair-pulling and torturing on my part, I got the band to play over the top of my demo.

Musically speaking, the song was unlike anything The Police had done to this point. A Caribbean vibe accompanies the song and though there are plenty of synths and piano parts, but they enhance the song and do not overtake it. Sting adds so much character with his voice and he plays some great electric double bass, which can really be heard in the drifting fade-out. Copeland's drumming is subtle during the verses, only accenting the hi-hat, but his lively, vibrant drumming on the choruses takes the song to another level and the outro segment, in particular, has him slamming his snare and adding loads of accents. While Summers doesn't have much to do, the song would not have sounded quite right with guitar parts. Sting's lyrics are romantic and self-deprecating.

Stewart told *Revolver* in 2000:

> I remember saying, 'Okay, put up Sting's original demo and I'll show you how crummy it is'. So Sting stood over me and waved me through all the changes. I did just one take, and that became the record. Then Andy did the same thing on the guitar. We just faced the music, bit the bullet, and used Sting's arrangements and demo. Damn.

Summers, for his part, simply said, '...as the guitar player I was saying, 'What the fuck is this? This is not the Police sound!' I think that sums up Andy's feelings quite well. It's hard to imagine all the torment over this song since it was clearly a gem and became a worldwide sensation, but at the time, Copeland and Summers were very frustrated and felt their roles were diminishing.

The music video was directed by Derek Burbidge who captured the band playing in front of a bunch of locals in Montserrat – they look either happy, bemused or both. The shots in the studio were filmed at AIR Studios, where the album was recorded (that studio was owned by Sir George Martin) and we see the guys dancing and prancing in the control room while having fun with the mixing desk. Copeland was quoted in the book *MTV Ruled the World* as saying:

> 'Every Little Thing She Does Is Magic' we shot in Montserrat, and it's strange how that was regarded as 'The Who destroying equipment of our time', because we were trashing that Trident desk. And that desk, by the way, ended up at Studio One in A&M, here in Los Angeles, and I've been to five or six different studios around the world that claim that the Neve sitting in their room is the one that we trashed. And I don't know which one is which. One Neve is the same as the other, if you ask me. And we weren't aware of trashing it at all. We were in the habit – because we were all very fit – of climbing over it, because it was very long. And if you were over there and you wanted to get over here to hit a fader or something, we'd just climb over it. Certainly, we were not cognizant of any abuse of the console. But we were just dancing around.

Needless to say, the video was on MTV around the clock.

Issued as the first single from the album in most territories (it was the second single from the record in the UK on 2 November 1981), 'Every Little Thing She Does is Magic' would soar to number one in Britain, number three in the US (staying on the charts for 19 weeks), number one in Canada, The Netherlands and Ireland, number two in Australia and made the top ten in Norway, New Zealand, Belgium and who knows where else. The song also went to number one on the US rock radio charts for two weeks and charted for a whopping total of 28 weeks. In the UK, the single received silver certification and charted a total of thirteen weeks.

This song might also set the record for the most 'e-oh's' in a single song (I have it at sixteen or seventeen) and it's all the better for it.

Perhaps the best way to finish discussing this song is via what Sting told Daniel Rachel for his book *Isle of Noises*:

> When I moved to London in 1975, I was struggling to make a living. I auditioned at the Zanzibar in Covent Garden. I sang 'Little Thing She Does Is Magic' (as it was called at the time) and the guy said: 'We need commercial hit songs. We don't need this kind of stuff'.

'Invisible Sun' (Sting)

By far the most political song from The Police at this juncture, 'Invisible Sun' was topical, controversial, atmospheric, sparsely arranged and quite bleak. It is also quite a stunning and harrowing listen. The song was inspired by Northern Ireland and the difficulties going on at that time, though it was easily applied to many other war-torn nations and the struggle to survive.

The song begins with an ominous, dreary synth pattern before Sting does a count in and Andy enters with a few guitar notes. Sting, of course, does a few 'whoa-oh, oh, whoa-oh's' to great effect. The drumming is simplistic, with Stewart nudging a tom drum, although Stewart's playing, in line with everything else, becomes more powerful in the chorus.

Andy lays down a short, flailing solo with ear-piercing notes up high on the neck before a return to the brooding verses and another chorus. The song then retreats to the intro music with the 'whoa-oh's' and Andy providing some more scathing lead lines. The creepy fade-out is chilling and The Police have outdone themselves once more.

In *Lyrics by Sting,* when talking about this song, he said:

> 'Invisible Sun' is a dark, brooding song about the lurking violence of those streets, patrolled by armored cars, haunted by fear and suspicion, and wounds that would take generations to heal. I'm happy that the glimmer of hope in the song's title was somewhat prophetic and pray that the sectarian violence that destroyed so many lives is well and truly over.

Stewart felt the song in a personal way as he told *Revolver:*

> For me, the song was about Beirut, where I'd grown up, which at that point was going up in flames. My hometown was being vilified by the media as a terrorist stronghold, and it was being blasted by bombs and napalm. Twenty thousand Lebanese were killed that year. And the Lebanese must have been feeling some heat from the invisible sun, because they were keeping their peckers up.

The music video was again directed by Derek Burbidge and was shot in black and white. Ghostly flashes of the band were briefly shown, popping in and out quickly. The images of war-torn Northern Ireland were quite stark to look at and the BBC banned the video, only assisting in the single's success as it soared to number two in the UK in September 1981 as the first single there. 'Invisible Sun' also went silver and spent eight weeks on the charts. Despite not being issued as a single in the US, the music video received heavy rotation on MTV in early 1982. This track was also issued in Ireland as a single and cracked the top five in that country.

Live, the song was a powerful number, and it was played by the band in 1986 on the *Conspiracy of Hope Tour* for Amnesty International, where they played the final three shows. It was an obvious choice, given the nature of that tour. With Kenny Kirkland on keyboards, this allowed Andy to focus on just guitars and not worry about Taurus pedals and guitar synthesizers. Bono of U2 came on to sing the last verse and chorus on the last two shows and blended in very well – being Irish, this subject was obviously important to him.

'Hungry For You (J'aurais toujours faim de toi)' (Sting)

An insistent, funky (and sensual) rocker, this song was sung almost entirely in French by Sting, who also played the sax parts on it. This was a track that Andy and Stewart sort of shook their heads at and just did what was needed.

Sting's solo demo was a four-minute instrumental and the basic framework was already there. For the album version, Stewart plays a mostly straight rock beat during the song, but occasionally stops for either rim shots or ride cymbals which add colour to what is a very repetitive track. The horns actually add some muscle and do not detract, while Sting is in complete control vocally.

Only once in a while does he sing in English, and even then, it's only for the line: 'No matter what I do, I'm still hungry for you'. The track is over in less than three minutes and is one of the only substandard songs on the album. It was performed on the 1981-82 tour with a horn section and not again afterwards.

'Demolition Man' (Sting)

The Police crank up the volume for this propulsive rocker, which is essentially the result of a one-take jam session based around a Sting solo demo he did in Ireland in 1980. Sting actually recorded another demo in early 1981 with Irish drummer Paul McAteer and handed off this demo to Grace Jones, who then recorded an artsy, bizarre, but very intriguing version of the song that could best be described as a mix of new wave, post-punk, funk and art rock on her album *Nightclubbing*, which came out in May 1981. The video was wonderfully strange and scored MTV airplay and some play in US dance clubs. Andy Summers told *Creem* magazine:

He [Sting] did have 'Demolition Man' previously, mind you – he'd already given that to Grace Jones to put on her *Nightclubbing* album. In fact, that was the song we recorded first. You have to break the ice with something, and that was an easy one to do. It's a very simple song. We all listened to the Grace Jones version and thought, 'Shit, we can do it *much* better than *that*'. It was a one-take job. To me, our version is more ballsy, which is what you'd expect from Grace Jones.

The Police version crackles with life right from the opening drum roll, as both Andy and Stewart jam with menace and Sting's horns add to the intensity. Summers attacks his 1961 Fender Strat with a litany of stinging solos that go throughout the entirety of the six-minute song. While Andy wails away, Stewart crazily pounds away on toms, snare, cymbals and anything else in his way. Sting keeps to the main riff on bass, stepping out of the way and allowing Summers and Copeland to slay the beast that is this demolition man he speaks of. Around the 5:49 mark, the song seems to end with Summers thrashing the whammy bar while Sting angrily honks the sax, but just as that ends, the band begin to jam again in the fade, which is audible for just a few seconds.

Although the majority of this song is instrumental, Sting comes up with some awesome lines such as: 'I'm a walking nightmare, an arsenal of doom, I kill conversation as I walk into a room'. This was actually the first song the band recorded for the album, as Summers mentioned, and it was one of four music videos from the album to air on MTV. Like the others, it was directed by Derek Burbidge and is simply the band playing the song in the studio in Montserrat. In concert, this song absolutely rocked and was played on some dates of the reunion tour.

Sting re-recorded the song in 1993 for the corny sci-fi film *Demolition Man* starring Sylvester Stallone, Wesley Snipes and Sandra Bullock. A decade earlier, in 1983, the Manfred Mann Earth Band covered the song on their album *Somewhere in Afrika* and got moderate MTV play with their synth-rock heavy version, which would also end up on their 1984 live album *Budapest*. No version can equal the one by The Police, but that Grace Jones rendition needs to be heard and seen!

'Too Much Information' (Sting)
Here's one with a dance/funk groove, lots of sax, wah-wah heavy guitar and some fat rhythms from Sting and Stewart. After the glorious snatch of wah guitar from Andy that starts the track, the bass grooves and a snap-tight snare comes in along with loads of horns.

Sting sings right along with the groove and the song quickly becomes an irresistible earworm. The song does tend to do the same thing over and over, but when you're locked into a groove this hot, you just roll with it. Sting's bass playing is fantastic here.

Andy gets a few lead lines in the fade, but sadly, he was rather underutilized on this cut. Sting's solo demo basically laid down what the song was going to be as he plays the majority of the instruments. This is an example of Sting's musical genius, but also of how dominating a figure he was becoming in the band.

The sog was coupled with 'One World (Not Three)' as a single for the clubs and peaked at number 60 on the US dance charts in November 1981.

'Rehumanize Yourself' (Copeland/Sting)

Sprightly verses and darker choruses shade this co-write by Sting and Stewart. This track is an example of how outstanding this band was with synergy as the drums, bass, guitars and sax all take a role and no one part outshines the other.

The track lyrically deals with the idea of how people can become disconnected from society or even themselves depending on the specific jobs we have chosen for ourselves. Careers like a policeman and factory worker are observed, but so are poor life choices like being a violent skinhead or member of The National Front, an English Fascist organization that was.

'Rehumanizing' oneself is trying to reconnect with society, decency and purpose – pretty heady stuff. Oddly it was used in the comedy *Bachelor Party* in 1984. There's an art to this track as the music coming out of the chorus is mysterious and the horns are low in the mix, but effective. An underrated track, 'Rehumanize Yourself', was not forgotten as it was surprisingly included on the 2007 double CD best-of *The Police* set, which was a strong seller tied into the reunion tour.

'One World (Not Three)' (Sting)

While every Police song has something stunning going on in the drum department, 'One World (Not Three)' definitely provides ample evidence as to why so many fans, critics and fellow musicians admire Copeland's man's playing. This track is probably the most reggae and ska-oriented on the album and it allows Stewart plenty of space to get creative.

After the opening hi-hat riff, the groove is instantly identified and Copeland's snare sounds crackling. His use of tom rolls and assorted off-beat fills is pure genius and he never forgets to return to the main beat. The bass, sax and guitar largely do the same thing throughout and Sting uses call-and-response vocals that made this designed for the live stage. This song would've easily fit in on either of the first two records.

Sting's message is on the money:

One world is enough
For all of us

There was a music video for this song, but it was rarely seen and was never played on MTV. It's the same as the other two videos showing the band playing in the dimly lit studio, just like the clips for 'Spirits in the Material World' and 'Demolition Man'.

'Omegaman' (Summers)

One of the absolute highlights of *Ghost in the Machine*, 'Omegaman' is the best song Andy Summers came up with for The Police. Initially titled 'I'm So Tired', Summers reworked the song after an early take by the band, which featured different lyrics and arrangements.

A&M Records wanted this as the album's first single, but Sting disagreed and vetoed it. This only added more tension and bad feeling within the band, but it was hard to argue with 'Every Little Thing She Does is Magic' as the opener.

In an interview with the *AV Club*, Summers was asked about this happening and recollected:

'Omegaman' was a really strong piece. A&M wanted to put it out as the first single. But Sting, who was feeling his power at the time, was freaked out. He didn't want it out. He refused. He got very upset, but A&M didn't want to upset him for all the typical reasons, so it didn't get put out. But that was A&M's choice. Miles took it to an A&M convention and he played it, and they went, 'This is totally the first single'. Which would have been great for me, but it didn't happen. That's the actual truth of it. At this point, who cares?

One thing we should care about is how excellent this song is. There's an eerie vibe to this one, and Sting is in excellent voice here, especially on the choruses. Andy's use of a guitar synthesizer here is fantastic and adds a lot of atmosphere. The solo section is especially intriguing, and his tones are truly effective in heightening the song's themes. At the time of the album's release, Summers told the magazine *Music U.K.*:

The first thing I had done was to go in and play a very nice Larry Carlton-type solo with the 335 – it was very nice, but for The Police, it was a little bit too ... derivative sounding, a little bit too straight. So I started again with the Multivox effects plugged up and I had the Roland guitar synth going through them. The duet on the synth was switched to a minor second apart, which is pretty excruciating (laughs), through a fuzz and something, and it just sounded incredible! I could see their hair standing on end in the control room; they couldn't believe this fucking sound that was coming over! And I was having great fun, in hysterics; it was like ten cats being strangled... course, finally Stewart and Sting came in, and there was dead silence, and they didn't like it. It was a bit too heavy for them. I was a bit disgruntled, so I went back. I started again and found a figure that really worked. So I sort of used the same sound, but I returned the guitar synth to fifths, I think, played the figure on the end, and it worked really nicely with a normal electric guitar playing the figure and the guitar synth. That went down a little better; I suppose it fitted the track a bit better. Not quite as hairy as the other one.

'Omegaman' is a dark horse favourite in The Police catalogue for many fans, and it's easy to hear why. It is such a shame Sting prevented it from being a single, but it doesn't taint the quality of the song a bit.

'Secret Journey' (Sting)
Perhaps the most atmospheric track on the album, this one features lots of guitar synth use (on the Roland GR 300) by Summers, including the ethereal introduction sequence which is solely Andy for about 50 seconds. The muted guitar notes for the verses are classic Summers and the chorus is surprisingly warm. Stewart's drumming carries the song to distant lands with lots of changes and Sting's bass is meaty. There's no solo, but a brief guitar synth pattern echoing the intro, which pops up again after the song fades at its conclusion. The way Stewart changes up his drumming is incredibly inventive, and his playing reveals more and more rewards with each song. The double tracking of Sting's vocal harmonies on the chorus is nicely done and the song proves to be yet another winner on an album full of them.

This unheralded gem was issued as a single in the US in May 1982 and climbed to number 46 on the charts and number 29 on rock radio, but deserved a much better fate. 'Secret Journey' has been largely forgotten about by the masses. Perhaps having a music video would've helped things. Only Australia and New Zealand would also give this as a single release.

The song was only briefly played live for a few dates in the US and dropped after that. Sting said the song was based on the 1963 novel *Meeting with Remarkable Men* by George Gurdjieff. In his book *Lyrics by Sting*, Mr. Sumner said: 'I was looking for some spiritual guidance in my own life and, after a few false leads, finally began to listen to the discrete language of my own heart'.

Melody Maker called the song 'the record's highest moment' in a review at the time of release and Summers himself called it his personal favourite, saying that 'I always thought it should have been a single'. (Meaning in the UK, of course!)

'Darkness' (Copeland)
This is pure art from the mind of Stewart Copeland; 'Darkness' is a ruminative song and it's simply stunning in both its expression and composition. Much like Summers writing his greatest Police song with 'Omegaman,' here Copeland comes up with his own finest Police song. It would also be used as a B-side to the 'Secret Journey' single.

As the last track on the album, 'Darkness' was a lost child in the annals of The Police discography, but now many fans and critics recognize how great this song is years later. Moody, mellow, contemplative and dark, the track features Sting on double bass and vocals and just a touch of sax low in the mix, Andy on traces of atonal guitar that is a perfect complement, and Stewart on drums and keyboards. The drums are very subtle (mostly just hi-hat) and there's a couple of rumbles of thunder for good effect. The piano and keyboard parts are prominent but just for accent, and the lyrics are much more introspective than we are used to from Mr. Copeland, which deal with fame and the drag that it can be. These lyrics both open and close the song:

> I can dream up schemes when I'm sitting in my seat
> I don't see any flaws till I get to my feet
> I wish I never woke up this morning
> Life was easy when it was boring

That line 'life was easy when it was boring' always stuck with me, even as a thirteen-year-old kid when I bought this album and was too young to truly appreciate what he was saying here – I certainly get it now. 'Darkness' is a fantastic ending to a fantastic album.

Ghost in the Machine Rarities
'Flexible Strategies' (Copeland/Sting/Summers)
The Police go funk and get down on this B-side, which they dusted off in about ten minutes. A&M wanted another B-side and this is what they got.

Summers does have a ripping guitar solo that sounds somewhat Middle Eastern and also jazz-inflected. The drumming is pretty wild, and the bass is rolling and large. Sax parts also punctuate the song, but if we are being honest here, this is not a particularly good piece of music. Copeland certainly seemed to agree, as he was quoted years later: 'Word came down from the marketing machine 'Create a B-side – today!' We walked over to the gear, strapped on, and played for ten minutes – a disgrace'.

Not quite a disgrace, 'Flexible Strategies' is nonetheless pretty forgettable, but the band had no choice but to crank out a product for the label, which is an utterly ridiculous way to do business, but that's the record industry for you. This track appears on both box sets and the rarities disc for the *Every Move You Make: The Studio Recordings* box set from 2018.

'Shambelle' (Summers)
Here is an excellent B-side that is quite worthy and a favourite amongst Police diehards. The song is instrumental and starts rather quietly with muted and clean guitar parts sounding a bit like XTC or Talking Heads before Copeland explodes on drums around the 1:40 mark and the track jumps out at the listener.

Things drop down again with a bass fill and some muted, jangly guitars and quiet drumming (mostly hi-hat and the occasional snare beat) before things leap up again. A low keyboard part also adds a touch of cinematic sound and Andy's awesome rhythm guitar work is on display. The mix is ultra-crisp and the drums sound incredible. Hugh Padgham is just a master of sound and his production work has stood the test of time for decades – even this instrumental B-side sounds spectacular. The song quietly fades out with a few jazz and blues runs by Andy and there it is. If this song had appeared on the album, it could've been developed with lyrics and worked even better.

In the *Message in a Box* liner notes, Andy said:

I'd just started writing some instrumental pieces then and it was an achievement to get Sting and Stewart to go along with it. I always thought the B-sides were the place where we had the chance to loosen up.

Stewart added:

Andy's songs were the most unconventional of all. It was a sad truth that most of our creative fire was activated by, and focused on, Sting's material around which we were building the sound of our group.

'Low Life' (Sting)

Although this was used as a B-side in the *Ghost in the Machine* era on the UK release of 'Spirits in the Material World', the song was actually recorded in 1979 during the *Reggatta de Blanc* era. Sting was fond of the song, but he seemed to be the only one.

Indeed, it's hard to imagine this on any Police album, but the guitar arpeggios are very pleasing and the bass (possibly a fretless) sounds great. The lyrics are not Sting's finest, leaning towards the snobbish. There's also a sax solo by musician Olaf Kubler whom Sting had met when working with Eberhard Schoener. The sax style here is pretty much pop/jazz and was out of place on a Police tune, especially for 1979, although ironically Sting would begin laying down sax on Police songs himself in 1981 (but in a way that worked in an alternative style for accents). Summers was not pleased as he reminisced in the 1993 boxset:

Neither Stewart or I liked 'Low Life'. I thought the lyric was snobby and it had a kind of corny jazziness to it. That jazz sax had absolutely nothing to do with The Police. Though in retrospect, well, it's not a bad song.

Stewart didn't quite have the same recollection as he said in the boxset liner notes:

But no! I always loved the song. It was one of Sting's coolest lyrics and the music was interesting. The only problem was that we were trying to identify our band sound and the sax solo – also very cool – was from a different genre.

Sting played this tune on his first solo tour and a very good version appears on his *Bring on the Night* live album. Branford Marsalis plays a great solo and Kenny Kirkland's keyboards add colour to the song.

'I Burn for You' (Sting)

This dark, spine-tingling work came from Sting's days with Last Exit, though in a much different form. This was yet another song that Sting recorded during his demo sessions in Ireland in 1980. The song was rejected for the *Zenyatta Mondatta* album and again missed the mark for *Ghost in the Machine*. A different version was then recorded for the soundtrack of the controversial film *Brimstone & Treacle*, written by playwright Dennis Potter, which Sting starred in.

The tension that builds in this song is palpable. Andy's guitar figures add texture and Stewart's percussive work is haunting. The verses are captivating enough, but when the bridge comes in, a soothing darkness envelops the song and Sting has layers of vocals come in that give way to some off-kilter guitar notes. Sting then delivers a singular acoustic bass riff that then becomes a ghostly chant, with Stewart going ballistic on a percussive assault, utilizing military snare, world music stylings and some jazz. The chants continue throughout and no more lyrics appear after the bridge.

But the bridge itself offers evidence of the lyrical intensity:

Stars will fall from dark skies
As ancient rocks are turning
Quiet fills the room
And your love flows through me
Though I lie here so still
I burn for you

'I Burn for You' is a Police song that does not get enough notice, but it is one of the most stirring moments in their canon. The band did a very rare performance of this song (albeit only the end section) coming out of 'Shadows in the Rain' during their appearance at the massive US Festival to over 250,000 fans in San Bernadino, CA.

Sting performed the song on his first solo tour in 1985, which is captured on the 1986 double-live album *Bring on the Night*. While the album version is very good, the version on the concert film of the same name, directed by Michael Apted, is jaw-dropping thanks to the sax work of Branford Marsalis and one of the most intense drum solos you'll ever see from Omar Hakim. It elevates the song to a level of sheer intensity, with a haunting beauty and darkness that is a perfect match.

The track also appears on the *Message in a Box* collection from 1993, along with the other two songs from the soundtrack the band recorded for the film. 'I Burn For You' did receive some FM airplay in the US, peaking at number

27 at rock radio in December 1982 and charting for nine weeks, though it was rarely heard again after that.

'How Stupid Mr. Bates' (Copeland/Sting/Summers)
Also from the *Brimstone & Treacle* soundtrack, this engaging instrumental piece has a shade of the Caribbean in its main theme, with squelching synths, marimba and Stewart's excellent touches on drums.
   That being said, it's just background music and obviously was composed quickly for the soundtrack. It is far better than the other instrumental for the film.

'A Kind Of Loving' (Copeland/Sting/Summers)
If you enjoy two minutes of someone screaming as though they're being tortured to the same lick played over and over, then you've come to the right place. A contender for the worst song under The Police name, this is really just an incendiary toss-off for the soundtrack.

'Don't You Believe Me Baby' (Sting)
This was a demo recording of a song that was first conceived during the Last Exit days in 1976, which was then revisited during the *Ghost in the Machine* era. It is an excellent song that is both danceable and laced with hooks and a new wave electronic sound that wouldn't have been out of place on a Human League, Duran Duran, or Ultravox album.
   It's Sting on bass and vocals with Jean Roussel on keyboards and programmed drums. The dark edge of the song is right within the feel of the material for the album, but perhaps Andy and Stewart didn't see any way they could work with the song, which is screaming for more development.
   This song has so much potential; it's a crime that it hasn't been properly recorded by Sting or The Police. The well-regarded Boston-based modern rock band Elsewhere covered this in 2017 on their EP *Multi-Man* – it's crackling with life, showcasing a modern sound that also pays debt to the original. The arrangements and the lead vocals are outstanding. The original Sting demo is a must-hear and so is this cover.
   Elsewhere, singer Michael Aroian told *Newswire.com*:

   I learned that it was a demo featuring the keyboardist who played on 'Every Little Thing She Does Is Magic'. I thought it was extremely cool and did a little research to learn that we could record it commercially as long as Sting and the publisher were credited. So when Elsewhere began working on the *Multi-Man* EP, I thought it could be a song worthy of being re-created. We love how it came out. The idea was to modernize it like the answer to the question, 'What would Sting, Andy and Stewart have done if the song had made their album?'

'Don't Think That We Could Ever Be Friends' (Roussel/Sting)
This was another demo from 1981 that is pretty much straight dance/pop with a synth beat. This is something The Police were wise to avoid, although it's easy to picture this cut on a Sting solo album from the 1980s.

It is by no means a bad song, it's just very typical of what a number of disposable pop acts would've done at the time. Sting's vocals are great on the demo, especially the better-sounding second take. This track sounds a lot like something Heaven 17 might've recorded at the time. It's just very hard to picture Andy and Stewart wanting anything to do with this.

Within a year, the song did indeed end up on an album when Dusty Springfield recorded it for her 1982 release, *White Heat*. Her version is pure dance pop/disco with synths, programmed drums, hand claps and weak guitars – Dusty's version isn't great. Incidentally, Roussel played on the Springfield album and wrote several other songs for the record, which itself disappeared without a trace.

'Don't You Look At Me' (Sting)
Here was another song that originated in the Last Exit days in 1976. This demo version showcases more of a smooth R&B/pop sound with lots of electric piano and soft synths from Roussel, which makes it sound like Michael McDonald-era Doobie Brothers – definitely inappropriate for The Police.

The keyboard solo is pure 1980s cheese with pitch bending on the synths; one wonders how Andy and Stewart managed to hold back from trying to clock Sting in the chops right then and there.

This isn't even a good Sting solo tune, but then again, it was probably just a scratch demo and Sting had no real intention of making this a Police song – at least one only hopes that was the case. The original Last Exit demo is an acoustic-based smooth jazz/pop-rock song that is far better than the 1981 demo. It's actually quite amazing hearing the Last Exit material and realizing that Sting had already found his voice at that point.

'It's Never Too Late' (Sting)
This moody song was one that should've made it to an album. Pulsing synths and bass and a racing programmed drum beat make this one sound like something from an 1980s action film or thriller. The chords are dark and brooding, as is this pulse and Sting's vocals are double-tracked on some parts. A song that might have been suitable for The Police, it may have even worked for a band like U2 or Simple Minds. This is an excellent song idea and it's very disappointing this one hasn't been worked up by Sting on his own or covered by someone instead. It's too good to be left by the wayside.

'Don't Give Up Your Daytime Job' (Sting)
This lighthearted, infectious pop/rock tune really needs to find a home someday. The track originated from Sting's Last Exit days and was written

on the day he left his job as a school teacher to try to make it in the music industry.

Musically, this sounds like a cross between Billy Joel, Andrew Gold and Supertramp. The Police could've made this a smash, although it is way too sunny for the *Ghost in the Machine* album and might've been better served on any of the first three albums than the latter two.

This song also sounds like it could've been the theme song to any number of corny 1980s TV sitcoms, particularly in the US.

Stewart Copeland, Andy Summers and Sting. Nobody can ever replicate The Police.

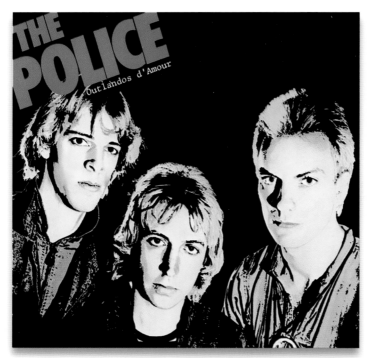

Left: The 1978 debut album *Outlandos d'Amour.* (*A&M Records*)

Right: *Reggatta de Blanc*, the band's first UK album chart-topper from 1979. (*A&M Records*)

Right: One of the most well-known songs of all time, 'Message in a Bottle' hit number one in the UK, but only managed number 74 in the US. (*A&M Records*)

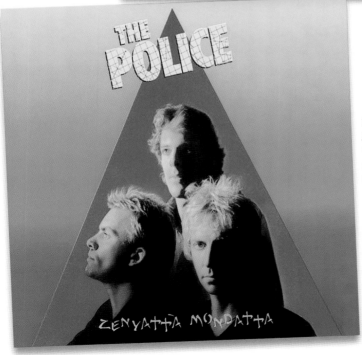

Left: 1980's *Zenyatta Mondatta* was another number-one album in the UK and went Double Platinum in the States. (*A&M Records*)

Left: The band's first foray into the world of music videos came with 'Roxanne' in 1978.

Right: The 1979 video for 'Message in a Bottle' was never used by MTV.

Left: 'Walking on the Moon' was the second straight number-one for the band. The video was shot at the Kennedy Space Center on 23 October 1979.

Right: The video for 'Don't Stand So Close to Me' was directed by Derek Burbidge and was another number-one UK smash.

Left: The video for 'Every Little Thing She Does is Magic' was shot in Montserrat, where *Ghost in the Machine* was recorded. The song was yet another UK number-one hit.

Right: 'Every Breath You Take' was a worldwide number-one hit in 1983 and the Godley & Creme B&W-shot video was an award-winner.

Left: *Ghost in the Machine* (1981) was a darker album and an even bigger success, selling over three million copies in the US. (*A&M Records*)

Right: 'Every Little Thing She Does is Magic' is magic, topping the charts in four countries in 1981. (*A&M Records*)

THE POLICE   SYNCHRONICITY

Right: The pinnacle: *Synchronicity*. The album sold eight million in the US alone in 1983 and spent 17 weeks at number one. (*A&M Records*)

THE POLICE

EVERY BREATH YOU TAKE

Left: The most-played song in the history of radio is 'Every Breath You Take'. And no, it's NOT a wedding song! (*A&M Records*)

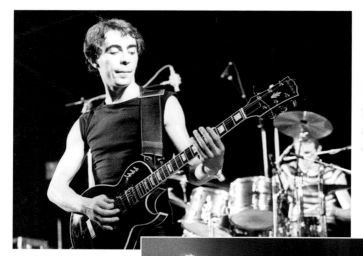

Left: Original Police guitarist Henry Padovani in action. (*Ian Dickson, Getty Images*)

Right: The first Police gig with the classic line-up on 18 August 1977 in Birmingham, UK. (*Getty Images*)

Left: A youthful Sting, Stewart and Andy. (*Richard E. Aaron/Redferns*)

Right: Sting in the BBC film *Brimstone and Treacle* in 1982. Not exactly a family night out!

Left: The night of the Strontium 90 gig in May 1977 with Mike Howlett. Yes, those shorts are unfortunate …

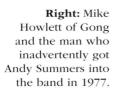

Right: Mike Howlett of Gong and the man who inadvertently got Andy Summers into the band in 1977.

Left: Released in 1986 just as the group broke up, this hits package included one new re-recording, which marked the end of the band's studio career. (*A&M Records*)

Right: *Greatest Hits* (1992) went Gold or Platinum in ten countries. Not bad for a band that had disbanded six years earlier. (*A&M Records*)

Left: A 1997 compilation featuring both Police and Sting solo hits. This includes a remix of 'Roxanne' by Puff Daddy. (*A&M Records*)

Right: Tied into the band's shocking reunion in 2007, this double best-of went Platinum in the UK and peaked at number three. It begins with the very first single 'Fall Out'. (*A&M Records*)

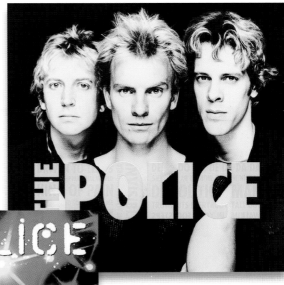

Left: *Live!* is the first official concert document of the band. It features two shows from 1979 and 1983. (*A&M Records*)

Right: The critically acclaimed four-disc set *Message in a Box* from 1993 is a rare box set that went Platinum in America and features tons of rarities.

Left: The exquisite *Every Move You Make: The Studio Recordings* box set was vinyl-only in 2018 before hitting CD a year later. (*A&M Records/Universal*)

Right: *Flexible Strategies* is a disc of rarities exclusive to the 2018 box set. Most had appeared elsewhere, but the 1983 reworking of 'Truth Hits Everybody' had never appeared on disc before. (*A&M Records/Universal*)

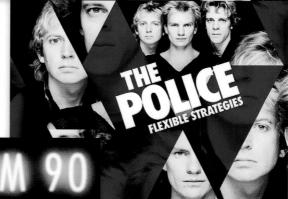

Left: The Strontium 90 recordings from 1977 finally got a legitimate release 20 years later. (*Ark 21 Records*)

Right: The reissue program began with a restored, expanded (and slightly edited) version of the 1980 documentary *Police Around the World* in 2022. (*A&M Records/Universal*)

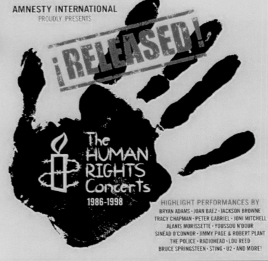

Left: *The Police Certifiable* is a fantastic 2008 double-disc, double DVD (or Blu-Ray) of a show in South America from the phenomenal 2007-2008 reunion tour. (*Cherrytree/A&M Records*)

Right: The 2013 *Amnesty International* box set features, what was thought to be, the last concert The Police would ever play on 15 June 1986 in East Rutherford, NJ. (*Shout Factory Records*)

Left: The 2007-08 reunion tour grossed over $358 million. To say the least, the guys reclaimed financial security.

Right: One of the world's most imaginative and explosive drummers: Stewart Copeland, pictured here on the reunion tour.

Left: Sting and Andy on the reunion tour looking distinguished and maybe even happy.

Right: An absolute genius on the guitar (not to mention photography and writing): Andy Summers.

Left: The adoration from the fans on the reunion tour was emotional every single night.

Right: Sting defies age, and don't we all wish we were Sting in some way?

Above: My ticket from the reunion tour in Philadelphia, PA on 19 July 2007. This $50 ticket would now almost certainly be at least $250 in 2024.

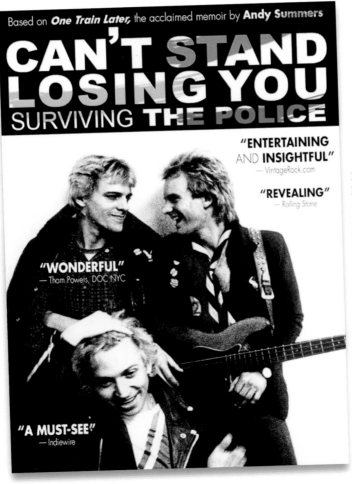

Left: Surviving The Police wasn't easy and it was also the name of this 2012 documentary based on Andy Summers' memoir *One Train Later*. (*Cinema Libre Studios*)

Synchronicity (1983)

Personnel:
Sting: bass, lead vocals, backing vocals, keyboards, saxophone, oboe, programming
Andy Summers: guitars, backing vocals, keyboards, lead vocals on 'Mother'
Stewart Copeland: drums, percussion, marimba, backing vocals
Released: 17 June 1983
Recorded: AIR Studios (Montserrat)
Produced by: The Police and Hugh Padgham
Engineer: Hugh Padgham
Cover Design: Jeff Ayeroff, Norman Moore
Highest chart position: UK: 1, US: 1, Canada: 1, Japan: 17, Germany: 4, Australia: 1

After completing the massively successful 1981-82 world tour for the *Ghost in the Machine* album, The Police broke off for a variety of individual activities. Sting starred in the aforementioned production of *Brimstone & Treacle* and even scored (much to his chagrin) a UK top 20 single with a cover of the late 1920s standard 'Spread a Little Happiness'. Andy teamed up with King Crimson guitarist Robert Fripp and they released a wonderful album on A&M Records called *I Advance Masked*, an eclectic mix of new age, alternative rock, fusion, world music and ambient music. It was quite avant-garde, yet also had a universal appeal due to the fact that pop and rock structures were also utilized. The album drew good reviews and placed in the US top 50 on the album charts. Copeland composed the score for the Francis Ford Coppola film *Rumblefish,* which was based on a novel by S.E. Hinton of *The Outsiders* fame. The score was very rhythmic and also featured found sounds. One song was on the soundtrack of *Rumblefish*, which paired Copeland with Stan Ridgway of the awesome US alternative new wave band Wall of Voodoo and was called 'Don't Box Me In'. This tune received some MTV support and college rock radio play in America and was a fun romp. The film and single were issued in 1983.

The Police had already begun working on *Synchronicity* in December 1982, and once again, they selected AIR studios in Monserrat. Hugh Padgham was on board again to produce and engineer and no other musicians would appear on the album. Tensions were running very high, especially between Stewart and Sting, with each band member recording in separate areas – Sting in the control room, Andy in the studio itself and Stewart in the dining room. Padgham diplomatically, and rather humorously, said this was done to obtain the best sound each instrument could get and for 'social reasons'.

This would be the album where synths are most prominent, though it did not overwhelm the end product. The Oberheim DSX sequencer was used, as well as a Roland Jupiter-8 and Prophet-5. The sessions were tense; Sting and Stewart could rarely be in the same room together and any overdubs were done with one member at a time due to the stress levels. When 'Every Breath

You Take' was being recorded, Sting and Stewart nearly attacked one another and Hugh Padgham almost abandoned the sessions.

Matters were not helped that both Sting and Summers saw their marriages coming to an end. Sting would also begin filming his role as Feyd-Rautha in the David Lynch-directed film epic *Dune*, which distanced himself further from the others and irritated Stewart. The three Godley & Creme-directed music videos for the album were monstrous hits on MTV, played as many as three or four times a day in constant rotation.

Synchronicity was released on 17 June 1983 and topped the US album charts for a mind-blowing seventeen weeks, going platinum eight times. In the UK, it went to number one and went platinum, whilst the album also hit the top in Canada, Australia and New Zealand, and number two in the Netherlands while racking up sales of over fifteen million copies sold worldwide. The album would chart for 75 weeks in America and 48 weeks in the UK.

Synchronicity was nominated for Album of the Year at the next Grammy Awards but was beaten out by Michael Jackson's *Thriller*, but won the award Best Rock Performance by a Duo or Group with Vocal. 'Every Breath You Take', which topped the US singles charts for eight weeks, was nominated for three Grammys and won two. *Synchronicity* was also placed at number 159 on *Rolling Stone*'s 500 Greatest Albums of all-time list, *Consequence of Sound* placed it at number 37 all-time, VH1 had it at number 50 on their *100 Greatest Albums of Rock & Roll*, and the album also was ranked at number 119 in the *Rock and Roll Hall of Fame Definitive 200*.

Synchronicity also was inducted into the Grammy Hall of Fame in 2009, and BBC Radio 2 had it at number 13 in a poll of listeners for *The Top 100 Favourite Albums* in 2013. In addition, when the decade of the 1980s was broken down, the album was placed at number 17 in *Rolling Stone* for the Top 100 Albums of the 1980s and it was voted Album of the Year in 1983 by readers of the magazine that year.

Pitchfork ranked it number 55 in its 2002 list of the 1980s Top 100 Albums, and *Q* magazine had the album at number 25 on its 2006 list of the *40 Best 1980s Albums* and it was also accorded a placement at number 91 in the *Virgin All-Time Top 1000 Albums* book.

The 1983-84 tour that kicked off on 23 July 1983 in Chicago, IL would break all box office records; the band weren't just filling arenas, they were now filling 50,000-70,000 seat stadiums.

When they played Shea Stadium in Flushing, NY (home of the New York Mets Major League Baseball team and also where The Beatles had famously played in August 1965, essentially starting stadium rock), Sting was later quoted as saying the band had reached 'the summit'. And, when you reach the summit, there's nowhere else to go, and the other band members knew Sting felt this way.

Box office records had been achieved and the band was now one of the biggest in the world. Ironically enough, this became something of an albatross around their collective necks; they never sought to be playing stadiums and they started feeling isolated as a result – this only increased the in-fighting and hostilities towards one another. Indeed, the band had reached the summit, and what goes up must come down ...

'Synchronicity I' (Sting)

The opening keyboard sequence accompanied by Stewart on ride cymbal lets the listener know that a bold new sound has been embraced by The Police, and once Stewart kicks in the full drum assault, the song is propelled into a pulsating, pounding rhythm you can rock out to – the music is intense and the beat doesn't let up. The song is dominated by Sting and Stewart, as Andy is recessed in the mix and just doesn't have much to do. He's contributing, however.

Sting worked this up as a solo demo in November 1982 in London at Utopia Studios. Lyrically, this is Sting getting very wordy and nerdy as the song is based on Carl Jung and his theory of synchronicity. The Swiss psychiatrist postulated an 'acausal connecting principle', whereby seemingly coincidental events were held to have an underlying relation. That, he believed, offered an explanation for ostensibly paranormal occurrences such as phone calls arriving from people just as we have been thinking about them, hence, synchronicity. Not your typical pop lyrics, eh?

This song not only opened the album but also each show on the 1983-84 tour. It was a radio hit in the US but was only issued as a single in Japan. When asked about the song by *Revolver* magazine, Copeland said:

I've had Sting up against the wall on this issue before, and he point-blank refuses to explain the connection. None of us in the band can even remember which one's which. The only way I can keep them straight is that 'Synch I' has Sting's cool sequencer part, that 'dunga dunga dung' thing that I, to this day, get all the credit for. People think it's me playing some percussive instrument, and I have to put them right. It was a real 'rama-lama' way of starting our set on tour, though it almost killed me to start with that kind of onslaught every night.

What's interesting is that originally this song and 'Synchronicity II' were to be linked together and here would be an extended instrumental sequence that was apparently rather trippy and progressive. Andy Summers said in an interview from 1983:

We had this section for 'Synchronicity', which we referred to as 'The Loch'. I went in and detuned my guitar synth to C sharp and it produced a great wash of sound, lovely. And there was an acoustic on top, a few cymbals and an oboe, really serene. We were going to have it at the end of 'Synchronicity I' – it was supposed to be the Loch Ness Monster – and then it would go into 'Synchronicity II'. But we couldn't really get it to work. Miles (Copeland) didn't like it ... it was too psychedelic for him.

'Walking In Your Footsteps' (Sting)

Sting gets a little corny here singing about dinosaurs (but he's not really singing about them now, is he?), yet this remains a quite interesting entry into the canon of The Police. World music surfaces as an influence here and Sting would explore this much further in his solo career. Thus, we get sounds of pan flutes and various African percussion, some of which Stewart also found with programming or played himself. The song is engaging musically, with Andy adding some guitar effects throughout, including some delay and harmonics that provide effective shading to the song.

Sting is singing in an affected accent about the possibility of humans becoming extinct – like the dinosaurs – but through nuclear destruction instead of natural causes. Essentially, he is seeing this as humanity's suicide. This is actually pretty clever, though it does come off as a little on the silly side with the analogy.

This also proved to be a fun concert piece and Sting seemed to really enjoy playing and singing it. This track is a long way from the likes of 'Next to You' and 'Fall Out', but if you listen back to songs like 'Masoko Tanga' and 'Reggatta de Blanc', it makes sense in terms of a natural progression.

'O My God' (Sting)

Sting had written a song with Last Exit called 'Oh My God', but this is not that song. However, a few of the lyrics from that song survived and found their way into this one, but that song bears no resemblance to the one that appears on *Synchronicity*. This 'O My God' starts a patchy set of songs on side one of the album that keeps the record from being a consistent one. However, that also adds to some of the charm in the fact that this track and the two that follow it are pretty left-field choices and add even more diversity to the overall album.

The song fades in with some guitar harmonics by Andy, Sting's funky bass, which sounds like a fretless, and some guitar synth washes. The first verse is fairly mellow, but once Stewart kicks things up on snare, the pace gets energetic. The song itself i feels more like some of the filler tracks from earlier albums. This is also a track that seems much more like a Sting solo song than a true Police song.

The lyrics are not Sting's best either, and when he sings, 'O my God you take the biscuit', it's especially cringe-worthy. Sting also wails on sax like a cat in heat on a summer night and it's not exactly tuneful. At least Stewart gets to jam and flail away on drums during the solo, but once the song ends and Sting plays a few mournful notes on sax, it's finally over.

Sting actually uses some lyrics from 'Every Little Thing She Does is Magic' towards the end and those are the best lyrical moments of 'O My God'. And after this song ends, thus begins one of the most notorious songs in Police history ...

'Mother' (Summers)

And now we have arrived at 'Mother'. This is one mom you apparently would not be sending Mother's Day cards and flowers to. This song has been debated since the release of the album in June 1983. The track sounds like a musical nightmare from Arabia and someone's destroyed psychosis being recorded in a torture chamber – and that's being kind.

If you put King Crimson, Throbbing Gristle, Frank Zappa, Sigmund Freud and a wounded animal in a recording studio, this might be the result. If you dislike or even despise 'Mother' this is understandable, and if you happen to like it, then you probably have to start explaining yourself.

Well, for one thing, it is demented and amusing. For another, it sounds like nothing else on the album or like much else anywhere. The lyrics are actually hysterical in a Norman Bates kind of way. This smothering mother sounds like a horror, much like in the Pink Floyd song of the same name from *The Wall* in 1979. Unlike the Floyd song, which has some beautiful melodies and arrangements, this song is nothing short of avant-garde soundscapes from hell. The guitars are scraped and angular and there's an oboe or sax being strangulated, adding to the madness. Summers cackles and howls in torment with twisted glee and neurosis.

How can you not have pity for this poor creature who is rambling these words to us all:

> Well every girl that I go out with
> Becomes my mother in the end

Of course, the guys were in on the joke. They knew this was pure theatre, but it was vintage Andy. Sting was never going to sing this, but he was won over and it ended up on the album. In an interview with *Songfacts.com,* Summers said:

> We all have our family situations, and I had a pretty intense mother who was very focused on me. I was sort of the 'golden child', and there I was, sort of fulfilling all of her dreams by being this pop star in The Police. I got a certain amount of pressure from her.

Andy's mum doesn't appear to resemble the character in the song and I'm not sure how she felt about this warped tribute, but the song has lived in infamy.

'Miss Gradenko' (Copeland)

Stewart Copeland's lone writing entry on the album was this two-minute track, which concludes a trilogy of songs from each of the three band members that can be seen as lesser cuts or even songs that should've been replaced on the album by B-sides or better songs that were not completed.

This is a wonderful little song. Andy's guitar arpeggios are delicate and there's definitely a Talking Heads vibe in there. Stewart's drumming is simply outstanding and as he always seems to know what to do, when his snare drums kick in, the song improves and his timing here is impeccable. Sting's bass playing is grooving and delightful, while his vocals are well-conceived. Andy's guitar solo is fantastic, offering jazz and fusion inflections and some nifty runs. The only gripe here would be that at two minutes long, it feels almost like a toss-off or throwaway, which it most certainly is not. Another set of verses or more choruses to get it to the two-and-a-half or three-minute mark would've sufficed.

The song seems to be some sort of spy thriller or espionage tale about a woman who either can't be trusted in her government job, or she can't trust the job itself and is trying to get out alive.

'Synchronicity II' (Sting)

A brilliantly conceived track that began as a Sting demo at Utopia Studios in November 1982, 'Synchronicity II' is arguably one of the top five Police songs. The music is intense, at times even a bit industrial and angry.

The tale involves two things going on that aren't actually connected but are happening at the same time symbolically, therefore occurring in a synchronistic fashion. In *A Visual Documentary* from 1984, Sting said:

> There's a domestic situation where there's a man who's on the edge of paranoia, and as his paranoia increases, a monster takes shape in a Scottish lake, the monster being a symbol of the man's anxiety. That's a synchronistic situation.

Indeed, it is, and so is the playing by the three musicians on this song, each of whom contribute significantly. The tale focuses on a man enduring a mind-numbing suburban life with both his domestic and professional life. The opening lines perfectly capture the setting at the start of each nightmarish day:

> Another suburban family morning
> Grandmother screaming at the wall

The grandmother (perhaps his mother-in-law) is losing her faculties and prone to screaming at the wall. Nobody in the family sitting at breakfast can even hear themselves because of it and it seems 'mother' (is this the man's wife?) is popping pills and threatening suicide. The kids probably aren't exactly well-adjusted, either. It's so awful that they can't even hear over the Rice Krispies in their cereal bowls – and that's just the start of the morning.

As the musical theme shifts to the driving pre-chorus, the mood intensifies and it's starting to get more than a little scary as we see the father starting to have a meltdown while at the same time something else is happening in a Scottish lake:

Daddy only stares into the distance
There's only so much more that he can take
Many miles away
Something crawls from the slime
At the bottom of a dark
Scottish lake

Not surprisingly, the day grows even grimmer for our poor protagonist and it's just one bleak image after another as the factory 'belches filth into the sky' and he walks past picketing workers like a zombie and has to listen to the secretaries whining yet again. What does he do? Nothing as Sting tells us – 'all he ever thinks to do is watch'. And whoever his manager or assistant manager is, it's an inferior individual who likes to belittle people, making it feel like 'a humiliating kick in the crotch'. And the tension keeps building, and elsewhere, the moving object in the loch is surfacing.

After screeching, atonal industrial noise from Andy's guitar where a solo would normally appear, we head to the final verses in which the man is heading home after another soul-sucking experience at work. It's quite apparent that he's going to snap now. And who hasn't felt like this at some point? A boss who is hideous to work for, rush hour traffic that only enhances the pain after a lousy day at work and a feeling of total despair and asking oneself: Is this all there is? And as we see in the last line, the man isn't exactly thrilled to be coming home to his family. Sting has some brilliant lyrics here to illustrate the point, especially when he references 'lemmings into shiny metal boxes' which obviously alludes to all the cars piled tightly on the highway just trying to get home and feeling like 'contestants in a suicidal race'.

The synchronicity that is happening is downright chilling and there's a sense of dread throughout with plenty of unresolved tension. I love the fact that we don't find out what happened in the end and it's just another aspect of the brilliance of this track.

Stewart's drumming is tight and crisp and he plays with very few fills this time around. The real star here is Andy, with his innovative and gruesome sounds. He decided to turn his amp up loudly and played directly in front of it. He couldn't actually hear what he was doing through the headphones, which probably made it even more effective. This is what you hear on the intro to the song, alongside some keyboard effects. Sting's vocals, including on the intro to the song, are incredibly effective and set the mood instantly.

Sting actually wrote this one and several others for the album while staying at Golden Eye in Jamaica, which was the former home of James Bond author

Ian Fleming. In *Lyrics by Sting*, we read Sting relating the atmosphere of where he was at when writing this song: 'Britain had gone to war with Argentina over the Falklands. Young men were dying in the freezing waters of the South Atlantic while I was gazing at the sunspots on the clifftop overlooking the Caribbean'.

I was always disappointed with the Godley & Creme video because it was just the guys playing in a giant soundstage outside of London in tattered clothes with trash flowing all around them from strong winds. Although there were some neat elements of this video, with each band member perched 25 feet above on separate towers looking like they were in a post-apocalyptic trash heap, it had nothing to do with the story of the song. It was on MTV constantly, anyway.

Issued as a single, the track hit number sixteen in the US and number seventeen in the UK as well as number twelve in Ireland, also falling just shy of the top twenty in Canada. At Album Rock in the US, the song would reach number nine and spent an amazing 31 weeks on the listings, which was a record at the time for most weeks of airplay on those particular charts.

'Synchronicity II' was always a powerful live number, and when Sting started playing it with his solo band in 1993, it exploded in a different way, with Dominic Miller ferociously playing guitar and Vinny Colaiuta adding intensity on drums.

The song has been covered a few times, most notably by metal acts. American prog-metal legends Queensrÿche did an excellent rendition on their *Take Cover* album in 2007, and Brazilian power metal band Angra tackled this on their *Secret Garden* album in 2014, also faring quite well.

'Every Breath You Take' (Sting)
And now we arrive at one of the most famous songs in music history, not to mention the most-played song in radio history, with over 15 million plays as of 2019. 'Every Breath You take' is also one of the most misunderstood songs in history, with many people actually choosing this as a wedding song. Do they even listen to the lyrics?

The song was written by Sting during his stay at Goldeneye in Jamaica and then demoed at Utopia Studios with Sting singing over some organ and piano. Sting composed the song after his marriage to Frances Tomelty was crumbling, and he was beginning his relationship with his future wife Trudie Styler, who just happened to be Frances's best friend. In 1993, Sting told *The Independent*:

> I woke up in the middle of the night with that line in my head ('every breath you take'), sat down at the piano and had written it in half an hour. The tune itself is generic, an aggregate of hundreds of others, but the words are interesting. It sounds like a comforting love song. I didn't realize at the time how sinister it is. I think I was thinking of Big Brother, surveillance and control.

In 2009, Sting told BBC Two: 'I think the song is very, very sinister and ugly and people have actually misinterpreted it as being a gentle little love song when it's quite the opposite'.

Sting brought the song to the band a few months after he did the solo demo and to say the least, he and Stewart did not share the same views on it. What's amazing is that Stewart did a stellar job at playing a simple pattern with that beautiful snare drum sound and slight cymbal accents. It's one of his greatest performances amongst many, because what he does here is beautifully restrained but not without some of his classic fills, including the crashing snare and cymbal with bass drum pedal at the end of each choral pattern in the song's lengthy fade. The arguments between Sting and Copeland were now getting most venomous and they often had to be separated from one another. Much like the other songs on this album, the band members recorded apart from one another, with Sting plugged into the recording console of the control room at AIR Studios, Stewart in the dining area with his drums and Andy in the main studio recording area.

The actual recording of the song only took about one week, but there was a big issue with the drums. The plan had been to get Stewart's drums finished in one take, but the drummer's busy playing wasn't to Sting's liking. Stewart struggled with getting the song right. In the end, according to Padgham, the drumming was pieced together from various takes; the snare was tightened as far as possible, the hi-hat used a 300-millisecond delay, the kick drum came from an Oberheim drum box and toms were overdubbed with mallets as were some of the cymbals. Hugh Padgham used an SM57 microphone to get that incredible snare sound but utilized different mics for the other parts, such as a Neumann 87S for the room mics placed about 10-15 feet apart. Without going into too much technical jargon, what you hear took a lot of work, as Padgham knew how special this song was going to be.

In *Classic Pop* magazine, Padgham recalled:

If Stewart couldn't be The Police's hit writer anymore, he wanted to show off his drumming skills. And he couldn't show off on 'Every Breath You Take'. One morning, Stewart came in and said, 'I've got an idea. I want to overdub a hi-hat on 'Every Breath You Take'. We got the hi-hat out, it's played on the song, Stewart goes skiing at lunchtime and Sting comes in going, 'OK, what fucking rubbish did you do this morning?' Everything Sting said about Stewart had an 'F' in front of it. I played him the new mix of 'Breath' with the hi-hat and Sting went, 'That's fucking *awful,* get rid of it'. I told him, 'If you don't like it, shouldn't you talk to Stewart about it?' The response came: 'No. It's my song. I hate it. Get rid of it. Now'. In those analogue days, if you got rid of something, it went to the great magnet in the sky. Sting stood over me, making sure I put the hi-hat track into the tape machine and wiped it. And, of course, Stewart comes in the next day going, 'Where's my fucking hi-hat?'

Padgham added:

> It wasn't that I wanted to take Sting's side over anyone else. I did it because I agreed with him. The problem with overdubbed hi-hats is that they often sound like overdubbed hi-hats rather than anything necessary to the song. We needed to get the album finished, and if the overdubs had got out of control, *Synchronicity* would have been like Brexit and never happened. It meant that, by the end of that album, I was not on Stewart's Christmas card list. We're fine now – I met up with them on the reunion tour, and Stewart is one of the loveliest, friendliest people there is.

Andy's guitar parts totally transformed the song. When it came to this track, Summers recalled:

> This was a difficult one to get, because Sting wrote a very good song, but there was no guitar on it. He had this Hammond organ thing that sounded like Billy Preston. It certainly didn't sound like The Police, with that big, rolling synthesizer part. We spent about six weeks recording just the snare drums and the bass. It was a simple, classic chord sequence, but we couldn't agree how to do it. I'd been making an album with Robert Fripp, and I was kind of experimenting with playing Bartok violin duets and had worked up a new riff. When Sting said 'go and make it your own', I went and stuck that lick on it, and immediately we knew we had something special.

Summers was right on the money on that fact. Copeland told *Mojo*:

> It was one of the most powerful songs he'd (Sting) ever written. Sting said, 'But we haven't got a keyboard player'. Andy said, 'Screw that!' so he and Sting fought. I agreed with Andy'. Stewart added: 'Sting did compromise his vision. He gave it up to Andy's unarguably brilliant guitar part. He surrendered.

Andy said in the same feature in the magazine:

> I took a moment to think: 'It mustn't be too vulgar. Big, brutal barre chords won't do. Mustn't get in the way of the vocals'. Then the track rolled and in one go, I played this succinct passage outlining the arpeggios, but with the added second or the major ninths which are beautiful when you drop to the sixth minor chord ...with his lick, I realize a dream that maybe I have cherished since first picking up the guitar as a teenager-to make something ... that guitarists everywhere would play ... and make my mum and dad proud.

Copeland also told *Classic Pop* magazine in 2020:

The demo was obviously a hit, but it was nothing like the current version, as Sting was singing the chords over a Hammond organ. Andy went, 'Guys, hello? We're a guitar band?' Andy is truly clever with harmony and worked out the song's arpeggiated guitar figure. One of our favourite in-band riffs is that, when Puff Daddy sampled 'Every Breath You Take' on 'I'll Be Missing You', he sampled Andy's guitar figure, not the melody or the lyrics. Me and Andy go, 'Go on Sting, pay Andy his royalties', and Sting will say, 'OK, Andy, here you are'... not reaching anywhere near his wallet.

His guitars are the glue to the song musically as they carry across the whole atmosphere created by the melody and lyric. Those stretched-out chords are very similar to what Andy used on 'Message in a Bottle' and you can even hear him sliding up and down the neck with his parts. Summers used a Fender Strat, Gibson 335 and a Roland guitar synthesizer for those subtle keyboard beds underneath. Sting's bass playing is also a key to the overall sound and he mixes in a Fender Jazz bass, a Steinberger and an upright electric bass, which we see in the music video and hear quite prominently in the space just before the 'I'll be watching you' part that segues into the repeating outro of choruses.

The bridge is the most powerful part of the song and transforms the mood, as simple power chords, beginning with F major, are played to incredible effect with dramatic feeling and potency. Then comes the single-note piano solo played by Sting (who also plays the piano chords), which is a drop-dead perfect choice. I've been a big fan of bridges, or middle-eights as some call them, and I've always stated that this is the best-conceived middle-eight of all time. Padgham actually recommended the single-note piano solo and it is more evidence of his exceptional abilities as a producer.

Apparently, Miles Copeland let Hugh know how important this song was by telling him: 'There's a goddamn hit if I ever heard one! Don't fuck it up, Hugh!' Padgham was later quoted as saying: 'I really think if my pet dog had produced 'Every Breath You Take', it would have been a hit'.

Not to be forgotten are Sting's vocals. Sting gave a brilliant performance that carried the mood and melody with class and care. There's nothing but sincerity in his voice. Sting told *Mojo*: 'It wasn't spontaneous. I planned exactly what timbre to sing it in, as a seductive song, a sexy song'. And indeed, it was seductive and famously misunderstood. 'Every Breath You Take' sounds sexy and sultry enough to be a wedding song, but any close analysis of the lyrics should give away the fact that this is anything but a warm and fuzzy love song. This should be clear right from the opening:

Every breath you take
Every move you make
Every bond you break
Every step you take
I'll be watching you

Those aren't the thoughts of a romantic; those are thoughts of a jealous lover and a stalker. Again, though, the way Sting delivers the song with his vocals and the musical accompaniment led by Andy's guitar arpeggios make it sound seductive.

The bridge is powerful and it's here where the lyrics are at their most romantic or sensual and only here. The sentiment is a lot different than the stalking lines, where the protagonist is almost voyeuristic. The bridge, or middle-eight as some refer to it, makes us feel sympathy for the jilted lover:

Since you've gone I've been lost without a trace
I dream at night I can only see your face
I look around but it's you I can't replace
I feel so cold and I long for your embrace
I keep crying baby, baby please

Then there's the music video from Godley & Creme. Striking in its black and white imagery, the video was inspired by a short film from the 1940s called *Jammin' the Blues*. The video isn't actually strictly in black and white, as there is a tint of navy blue. There are a lot of excellent camera shots and angles used on all three band members. A piano player and string section also appear, but they are just to enhance the video as there are no strings and Sting played the piano parts. The video cost around £70,000 ($100,000) but was well worth the investment, as it would win an award for Best Cinematography at the 1984 MTV Video Music Awards.

And why is there a window washer in the video? Kevin Godley explained to *Songfacts*:

The window washer felt right for that kind of noir feel. But, it also may be somebody who you don't expect to be watching the process, which refers to that sense of surveillance that the song is really about. We specifically did not want to know his story. That's something I've held fast to all the years I've been doing this: I hate telling the story of the song, because it's either show or tell -- it's not both. If the song is saying something, you don't want to be showing what the song is saying. You want to be putting the performance of the song; something about the song, in a place, a frame if you like, that enhances the experience. Don't do the obvious. But, in this case, I think the window cleaner is perhaps a suggestion of somebody watching.

'Every Breath You Take' was issued on 20 May 1983 and topped the US singles charts for eight weeks and the album rock charts for nine weeks. The song would also reach number one in the UK for four weeks and hit the top slot in Canada for four weeks, and in Ireland, Israel and South Africa, it also went to the top slot. A number two placing was achieved in Australia,

Norway, Spain and Sweden. The top ten was also where the song went in Austria, Belgium, Denmark, Finland, France, The Netherlands, New Zealand, Poland and Switzerland. The single earned platinum sales in the UK and went gold in the US, where it also charted for a hefty 22 weeks.

In 1983, the song was voted Song of the Year in both the fan and critic polls for *Rolling Stone* and was the number one-selling single of the year in the US, becoming the fifth-best-selling single of the 1980s in America as well. 'Every Breath You Take' is also ranked number 25 on the *Billboard Hot 100 All-Time Top 100 Songs* list. In 2015, a public poll in Britain by ITV had it as the number-one song of the 1980s.

At the 1984 Grammy Awards, 'Every Breath You Take' was nominated in three categories and won in two: Song of the Year and Best Pop Performance by a Duo or Group with Vocals. In 1983, Sting won the Ivor Novello Award for Best Song Musically and Lyrically. The song is also in the Rock and Roll Hall of Fame. Sting makes more than £1,400 ($2,000 US dollars) each day just from this song alone, and in May 2019, it knocked off 'You've Lost That Lovin' Feeling' by The Righteous Brothers as the most played song in radio history.

There have been hundreds of covers of the song, though not very many of them were any good. It's just an impossible song to try to improve upon. There are a few good covers of note, though. Quality takes on the song include ones by UB40, Everclear, Postmodern Jukebox with vocalist Vonzell Solomon (who brings down the house with her soul and gospel chops) and Joan Osborne. The classical/pop duo 2 Cellos also did a highly unique take that is quite splendid, actually and will probably get played at weddings for years to come. At this point in time, 'Every Breath You Take' can easily be considered a standard as much as 'Moon River', 'As Time Goes By' or 'Fools Rush In'.

In 1997, the song was prominently sampled on the Puff Daddy/Faith Evans smash 'I'll Be Missing You' (dedicated to the late Notorious B.I.G.), which went to number one in the US for eleven weeks and won a Grammy. Sting would perform the song with Puff Daddy at the MTV Video Music Awards later that year. Despite the fact the sample was based on Summers' guitar riffs and Sting isn't even featured on the song, it was Sting as sole publisher who received the financial windfall.

Summers amusingly summed it up:

The Puff Daddy one was weird for me, because, I mean, what do you use with the guitar riff? He actually sampled my guitar, and that's what he based his whole track on. Stewart's not on it. Sting's not on it. I'd be walking round Tower Records, and the fucking thing would be playing over and over. It was very bizarre while it lasted.

'King Of Pain' (Sting)

This pop masterwork was another song that Sting demoed solo in 1982 at Utopia Studios and had written while staying at Goldeneye, as he did for many of the songs on this album. Going through a separation, feeling the animosity from his friends because he was having an affair with his wife's best friend (who would become his future wife), and also feeling misery from his bandmates, Sting came up with the idea of being the 'king of pain'.

In *Lyrics by Sting*, he relates this tale:

I was sitting moping under a tree in the garden, and as the sun was sinking toward the western horizon, I noticed that there was a lot of sunspot activity. I turned to Trudie. 'There's a little black spot on the sun today'. She waited expectantly, not really indulging my mood but tolerant. 'That's my soul up there', I added gratuitously. Trudie discreetly raised her eyes to the heavens. 'There he goes again, the king of pain'.

Though the song is five minutes long, it does not lag at any one point and is lyrically and musically intoxicating. The imagery that Sting uses is rich, verbose and detailed, whilst the music is varied and highly unusual for what is supposedly a pop/rock song. The key line that Sting states throughout, 'There's a little black spot on the sun today', is certainly a bleak image, but a poetic one as well.

Andy's choppy guitar lines are beautifully realised, as is Stewart's variety of percussion, and Sting creates different textures through a mix of a Steinberger and an electric upright bass. A hint of xylophone (played by Copeland), marimba and piano are utilized with artful taste and creativity. The sonic overtones are sublime and there are also spaces that breathe, making this yet another artistic triumph.

Sting also borrowed from Jung and Koestler for his lyrical inspiration and there are some seriously amazing visages created by Sting's lyrics:

There's a king on a throne with his eyes torn out
There's a blind man looking for a shadow of doubt
There's a rich man sleeping on a golden bed
There's a skeleton choking on a crust of bread

And yet, Sting and the band somehow craft all this verbiage and make it irresistibly catchy. No wonder that the song was another major hit as a single, soaring all the way to number three on the US charts in the summer of 1983 (also reaching number one at album rock radio for two weeks without the aid of having a video) and also reaching the number one position in Canada and making the top ten in Ireland. Curiously, the song wasn't issued in the UK until early 1984, peaking at number seventeen and would only reach number 44 in Australia. The single also racked up 16 weeks in America on the singles charts.

Though there was no music video for the song, a video was cobbled together for the Australian market when the single was issued there as the band toured Down Under in early 1984. The video was actually a collection of clips from the short promo film *Studies in Synchronicity* and was not anything new.

There have been a few covers of the song, including Alanis Morissette in 1999 for her *MTV Unplugged* album and – most hilariously – Weird Al Yankovic remaking the song as 'King of Suede' in 1984 for his album *Weird Al Yankovic in 3-D*, which was quite amusing and hit number 62 on the US singles charts. In Al's version, a clothing store owner is the 'king of suede' and Al actually did research for the song by going to clothing and fabric stores and taking notes. He claimed he got a 'lot of nasty stares from store managers'. If that isn't the ultimate homage to The Police, I don't know what is.

'Wrapped Around Your Finger' (Sting)

How many top ten singles namecheck Mephistopheles, Scylla and Charybdis and also use words such as alabaster, fruition and tuition? One would be the answer, and it's 'Wrapped Around Your Finger' from The Police. It's as though Sting was educating us all and entertaining us at the same time.

This song was issued as the second single from the album in the UK in the summer of 1983 and was chosen as the fourth single in the US in the winter of 1984. Despite the wordiness and artsy nature of the song, it became a big hit, reaching number eight in the US (charting for a total of 16 weeks overall) and number seven in the UK, as well as earning placings of number ten in Canada, number five in Spain, topping the charts in both Ireland and Poland and also scoring the top twenty in The Netherlands and Germany. At US album rock radio, it would peak at number nine and charted for a whopping 27 weeks.

The song is quite seductive and uses a variety of instrumentation, including various keyboards, marimba, xylophone, guitar synthesizers and percussive instruments such as mallet, gong and chimes. The guitars are quite faint but add a flow to the music and Stewart is quite diverse in his arrangements, which are subtle, yet technical. It's not until the 3:30 mark that he truly uses any drums when he changes the tempo with a thwack of the snare and gets in some lovely fills before the song begins its hypnotic fadeout.

A challenging piece of music, it was as sophisticated a pop song as could be, but still had so much charm and elegance that most music lovers didn't bat an eyelash at how complex the structure was, and somehow mass appeal was attained once again by the band. With Sting referencing Greek mythology and mentioning the devil himself (Mephistopheles), it was quite obvious that the band's audience had grown up just as the band had and Sting could pretty much get away with any of his literary references or using his thesaurus for lyrical content.

The Godley and Creme video was another artistic triumph and quite unique. Though the video was shot in slow motion, the actual lip-sync was still in time with the music, making for a highly unusual look. Add to the fact that the band was surrounded by a maze of lit candles and it was very absorbing to the visual senses. Godley told *Songfacts* the following:

> I had the mad notion that wouldn't it be interesting if somehow the film was exclusively in slow motion, but the lip-sync was somehow in time to the music. We sat down and thought about how this might be possible. You see it quite often nowadays, but I think this was the first time it was ever done. In the studio, we played a sped-up version of the song, so the actual environment we were working in was totally opposite to what it ended up looking like – it was Mickey Mouse. You were listening to Mickey Mouse singing 'Wrapped Around Your Finger' at double speed. We were shooting at 50 frames per second, the idea being when you slowed the film down, they were moving in slow-mo but they were in sync with the track at real time. And it did work. Not perfectly, but it looked amazing – it looked really, really amazing. But on the day, it was insane, because they were rushing around and hitting drums and playing guitars and singing at double speed. It was manic, and by the end of the day, they were exhausted.

Also amusing was the sight of Summers prancing around with an acoustic guitar, an instrument that didn't even appear on the song and in fact, would never appear on any Police song. Summers didn't hide his feelings on the song and the video in the book *I Want My MTV*: 'I was kind of pissed off about that one. I've never been much of a fan of that song, actually. Sting got to shoot his part last in that video and made a meal of knocking all the candles out. Fuck him'.

'Tea In The Sahara' (Sting)
The album closes with an atmospheric number inspired by the Paul Bowles novel *The Sheltering Sky,* which moved Sting quite a bit. 'Tea in the Sahara' is actually the name of one of the chapters in the book where the character Port is told a story in which three sisters wait for a prince to join them in the Sahara Desert, but he never shows. The book was turned into a film in 1990 by the legendary director Bernardo Bertolucci but was a box office bomb, grossing only two million dollars on a budget of 25 million dollars.

In the mid-1990s, on a CD-ROM that was released and included a Sting interview, he stated:

> Paul Bowles has written very many books, but he wrote a book called *The Sheltering Sky,* which became a film by Bertolucci, a few years ago. I read it long before it was a film. It's one of the most beautiful, sustained, poetic novels I've ever read. It's about Americans that regard themselves as travellers and not tourists, and I class myself in that category. I'm a hopeless tourist, but I'm constantly on the move.

The song features lots of soundscapes and eerie guitar clipping, intimate percussion, guitar that sounds like some of Robert Fripp's interesting Frippertronics, and buoyant bass, with Sting delivering one of his best vocals on the album and even laying down some oboe at the end. It's an awesome way to close out the album and a perfect driving song or song to listen to at night. Summers explained his role in the song to *Guitar World*:

> On 'Tea in the Sahara' I used what I call, tongue in cheek, my 'wobbling cloud' effect. It comes with using a highly overloaded guitar, to the point of feedback, and moving the chord off just as it's about to break. It's a sound I do a lot in concert, this sort of echo guitar, where basically I turn most of the signal off so that all you hear is echo. Then you control it with the volume pedal, so you just hear this floating, shimmering sound. And you've got to play the right chords, you can't play G major or D7 – it sounds cruddy. You've got to play space harmonies to make it more like that – triads with open strings, tended harmonies like 9ths and 11ths, 27ths. It's really all by ear.

This song would appear on an episode of the hugely popular US TV crime drama *Miami Vice* in 1985 and a live version was used as the B-side to the UK release of 'King of Pain' in 1983 and included on the *Message in a Box* collection in 1993. Issued as a single only in Poland, 'Tea in the Sahara' would reach the top ten there. The song was also included on the double-CD compilation album *The Police* in 2007, which was tied into the reunion tour.

Synchronicity Rarities
'Murder By Numbers' (Sting/Summers)
A diabolic work of genius, this song was actually on the *Synchronicity* album for some people such as me, who, as a thirteen-year-old old, bought it on cassette and got this as an extra track at the end. It did not appear on the original LP or CD release in 1983.

This song is very worthy of being dubbed a Police classic and features some wicked lyrics and amazing music to accompany it. This rather sinister track was developed at AIR Studios and was allegedly done in just one take. Indeed, it has a loosely structured feel and sounds live, especially the raucous ending where Stewart goes ballistic on drums.

A jazzy feel pervades throughout and Andy's delectable chords carry the song. He uses some unusual chords and intervals that make the song as mysterious as the lyrics. Sting's vocals are dead-on and the lyrics are cutting; his melodies act as walking bass lines and he vamps away with some jazz vocals. Each line is sly and devious and one can picture him in a black turtleneck with white gloves and librarian's glasses, turning to the camera with a sly nod as though it was he who got away with the murder.

In particular, I love the last set of verses and chorus because Sting has tapped into the evil subconscious and ruthlessness of the human mind:

> For murder is the sport of the elected
> And you don't need to lift a finger of your hand
> Because it's murder by numbers, one, two, three
> It's as easy to learn as your ABC's

Stewart's drumming is in some crazy time signatures and the whole song shows how ingenious these three guys were. This song is seriously intense and yet it was cut in one take and sounds effortless. The chemistry of the band is uncanny. A song like this shows where Sting was headed in his solo career in terms of jazz. The song is highly regarded in The Police canon by fans, critics and fellow musicians.

In 1988, Frank Zappa covered the song on his *Broadway the Hardway* album and Sting did a hilarious satirical intro to the song before singing it with Frank's amazing band. Sting later said he was nervous as hell being on stage with Frank and who could blame him? All went very well, though and it was funny hearing Frank introduce him as 'Mr. Sting'.

In 1995, a psychological thriller that was rather good called *Copycat,* starring Sigourney Weaver, Holly Hunter, Dermot Mulroney and Harry Connick Jr. (who plays an evil role), was released in theatres and became a moderate hit. In the film, a serial killer leaves the lyrics to The Police song as a clue.

The twisted 2002 hit psychological thriller *Murder by Numbers,* starring Sandra Bullock, Ryan Gosling and Michael Pitt, was named after this song as well. This only enhances the fact that 'Murder by Numbers' has earned its wicked reputation as well as a lot of respect.

In *Lyrics by Sting*, the song is described by 'Mr. Sting' while he was still on the Caribbean island of Montserrat and he took a tape of the chords with him (that Andy had played) on a long walk to a volcano at the top of the island:

> A few years later, this volcano would destroy half of Montserrat, but on this
> day, it was just bubbling quietly and throwing up a strong smell of sulfur.
> The words formed in my head and that pungent smell of sulfur continued
> to cling to the song: Jimmy Swaggart, the TV evangelist, publicly cited it as
> an example of the devil's work. He condemned it colourfully while entirely
> missing its irony and its satirical content.

'Murder by Numbers' was played live on the 1983-84 tour (and just a few shows on the reunion tour) and went down very well with audiences. Incidentally, the sarcastic handclaps heard at the end of the song were done by roadies Danny Quatrochi, Jeff Seitz and Tam Fairgrieve. They were instructed not to clap with any enthusiasm so as to give off the impression of a small, unimpressed club audience.

'Someone To Talk To' (Summers)
If Andy Summers was to only get one song on *Synchronicity*, was Sting using some sort of twisted reverse psychology by choosing 'Mother'? Was Sting trying to hide Andy's true talents as a writer by not allowing 'Someone to Talk To' on the record but inflicting 'Mother' upon an unsuspecting world? After all, there is no song more polarizing in the catalogue of The Police, and I wouldn't put it past Sting to be sitting there grinning and saying, 'See? I told you so! That's why I write everything and call the shots!'

Synchronicity would not be the same album without 'Mother', however, and I'm glad it's there because it's a delight of musical and psychological horrors. 'Someone to Talk To' is a very good song, though and it would've made the album even better for its inclusion.

The song slides along quite nicely and sees a distinct ska and reggae undercurrent prevail while Andy sings quite effectively in a lower register, sounding quite like a mix of Benjamin Orr of The Cars and Adrian Belew of King Crimson. In fact, this really sounds like a Belew song and could easily have been on any of the 1980s King Crimson albums. That is understandable, seeing as Andy had been recording with Crimson leader Robert Fripp.

The song was demoed by Andy at AIR Studios and was originally titled 'Goodbye Tomorrow' with different lyrics and some musical parts – including Sting on sax – that ultimately were not used. Some guitar solos were also removed from the demo.

Summers' lyrics are actually quite good, detailing a disintegrating relationship and the regret that follows.

'Someone to Talk To' was used as a B-side to the 'Wrapped Around Your Finger' single in the UK and 'King of Pain' in the US and was included on both box sets in 1993 and 2018.

'Once Upon A Daydream' (Sting/Summers)
The B-side to the 'Synchronicity II' single, this song was a Sting/Summers co-write during the *Ghost in the Machine* period and is an excellent composition. The chords are very intriguing and the lyrics are cinematic and captivating. This song deserved a proper place on an album, but it did eventually find a home on both box sets.

Summers came up with the chord sequences and Sting added the lyrics to fit them while he was catching some sun by the swimming pool in Montserrat. The chords are evocative and moody and there are some fat keyboard paddings used that sound like a twisted carnival, and when the song hits the chorus, it elevates to a dreamy level. No Police song really sounds like this and the lyrics tell quite a tale, which at times is downright disturbing. Sting took some real chances with these lyrics and they sound like they'd fit some of the film noir flicks that he was in.

The opening seems innocuous enough with the following introduction to the tale:

Once upon a daydream I fell in love with you,

Afterwards, things take an extremely morbid turn by the second verse:

Once her daddy found out,
He threw her to the floor
He killed her unborn baby,
And kicked me from the door
Once upon a nightmare I bought myself a gun
I blew her daddy's brains out,
Now hell has just begun

What the hell has just happened here? By the final verse, it seems that this 'daydream' turned out to be anything but:

Once upon a lifetime,
A lifetime filled with tears,
The boy would pay for his crime,
With all his natural years,

The final chorus goes to the fade ominously saying: 'Once upon a daydream, Doesn't happen anymore, Once upon a moonbeam, This is no place for miracles'.

Collaborations like this one between Sting and Andy were few and far between by this point of the band's career, but more of these moments should've happened when you get results as creative and good as this. Sting was fond of the song, stating in the *Message in a Box* liner notes: 'I love it. It's a set of chords that Andy came up with and I wrote them by the pool in Montserrat. It's very dark, but that was the *Ghost* period – pretty intense'.

Stewart had a fantastic quote about this song and Sting in general: 'Most people would lounge and bask in the sun by a swimming pool, but Sting would create a cloud around himself and stare grimly at the horizon while he organized his dark thoughts into beautiful music'.

The Police Hiatus And The Guys Fly Solo

In 1984, with the other members very busy on other projects and Sting donning his codpiece in *Dune* and contributing to 'Do They Know It's Christmas?' for Band Aid, it was quite obvious that the Police were put on hold. There was quite a lot of speculation at the time that The Police were finished, though there was no announcement as such. Sting achieved phenomenal success with his debut solo album *The Dream of the Blue Turtles,* in 1985 and toured for the first time as a solo artist as well as appearing at *Live Aid*. There would be a return from The Police in June 1986 for the Amnesty International concerts on the Conspiracy of Hope tour, but sadly not for long.

Sting achieved massive solo success and his first four albums were truly wonderful. After that, it was a decline into largely forgettable adult contemporary, an orchestral album of re-recordings, a Christmas album (or rather a seasonal album as Sting called it), a re-recordings album, an album of duets, Disney songs and ... an album of lute music?

After his debut album, Sting continued an incredible run with 1987's ... *Nothing Like the Sun*, 1991's *The Soul Cages* and 1993's *Ten Summoner's Tales*. It was only with the 1996 album *Mercury Falling* that Sting began drifting towards material that was a bit blander and more saccharine. *Brand New Day* was an improvement in 1999, but 2003's *Sacred Love* continued the creative malaise, which he hasn't really moved away from, though each of the albums have some positives. In 2006, Sting baffled the public and did an album of lute music titled *Songs from the Labyrinth* – the less said about that one, the better. At least that drove him to the reunion of The Police in 2007-08.

In 2009, Sting made a seasonal album – which was a nice twist on the overdone Christmas album concept – called *If on a Winter's Night ...* and then hopped on the orchestral bandwagon for 2010's *Symphonicities*. Sting returned with a more creative album in 2013 titled *The Last Ship*, which was based on ideas going back to *The Soul Cages* and became a Broadway musical in 2014, collecting two Tony Awards the following year. A proper studio album called *57th and 9th* arrived in late 2016 and finally saw the man returning to his rock and pop roots. The muse was gone with the next few releases, however, which were an album of re-recordings in 2019 (*My Songs*) and an album of duets creatively titled *Duets* in 2021, both offering something of a K-Tel compilations-type vibe. No matter, though. Let's also note that Sting has been nominated for an insanely impressive 45 Grammys and won 17 times.

Sting also had an acting career and while he was rather good both on film and on stage, he was in some truly hideous cinematic debacles like *Brimstone & Treacle, Plenty, Stormy Monday* and *The Bride*. We mustn't forget Sting's major role in the expensive sci-fi epic *Dune* in 1984. In the film, Sting played the character of Feyd and his infamous line of 'I. WILL. KILL. HIM!' in the final battle has lived on in cinematic lore.

Sting has also appeared on and off Broadway and done a litany of charity work. Mr. Sumner is an icon and a talented and very funny, intelligent man and a genuinely good guy. He was also fantastic at both the *Live Aid* and *Live 8* concerts and the *Amnesty International* tours of 1986 and 1988. Add in the loads of charity work and the pleas for the rainforests and Sting is quite the man of all seasons.

Stewart Copeland has had a distinguished career doing numerous film and television soundtracks and among his best scores are for *Talk Radio, The Leopard Son, Wall Street, Surviving the Game, The First Power, Men at Work, Hidden Agenda* and yes, even *Good Burger*! Stewart has an amazing 45 film scores to his credit. He has also scored operas and ballets and done sessions with Peter Gabriel, Tom Waits as well as others and did collaborations with Stan Ridgway of Wall of Voodoo ('Don't Box Me In' from *Rumblefish* in 1983) and Adam Ant ('Out of Bounds' from the film of the same name in 1986), both of which were college rock and MTV hits.

Copeland was part of the semi-supergroup Animal Logic with bass legend Stanley Clarke and singer Deborah Holland, who did two albums in 1989 and 1991, and the jam-band supergroup Oysterhead with bassist/vocalist extraordinaire Les Claypool of Primus as well as guitarist/vocalist Trey Anastasio of Phish. Oysterhead issued *The Grand Pecking Order* in 2001 and toured that year, making one appearance in 2006 at the Bonnaroo Festival. Stewart also briefly joined The Doors (Ray Manzarek, Robby Krieger, Ian Astbury of The Cult on vocals and bassist Angelo Barbera) in 2002 and appeared on *The Tonight Show* on US television with the band, but he suffered an arm injury after falling off a bicycle (when Stewart falls off of moving objects and damages his arm, bands usually crumble and acrimony follows) and was suddenly no longer in the group which led to a flurry of lawsuits.

Stewart also directed the Police documentary *Everyone Stares: The Police Inside Out* in 2006, which drew acclaim, and played at the *Sundance Film Festival*. Stewart has remained busy with classical music, opera, his own YouTube channel – where he plays with other musicians – and writing his memoirs, as he did with the book *Strange Things Happen: A Life With the Police, Polo and Pygmies* in 2009. In 2017, he became part of another all-star collaborative called Gizmodrome with ex-Frank Zappa, King Crimson, David Bowie man Adrian Belew on guitar and vocals, Italian keyboardist Vittorio Cosma and Level 42 bass wizard Mark King. They released a self-titled album that same year. Oysterhead became active again in 2019.

In 2021, Stewart announced an album with Grammy award-winning artist Ricky Kej for release in July 2021 titled *Divine Tides,* following that up with *Police Beyond Borders* in 2023. He also released a delux version of his Klark Kent material in 2023, alongside the *Spyro* album in 2022. *Police Deranged For Orchestra* was also released in 2022.

Andy Summers also has had a distinguished career. Like Stewart, he has also done plenty of film scores, including *2010: The Year We Make Contact,*

Rumble Fish, Down and Out in Beverly Hills and *Weekend at Bernie's*.
He had his greatest commercial success collaborating with King Crimson
guitar legend Robert Fripp on the albums *I Advance Masked* (1982) and
Bewitched (1984). Summers has released 14 solo albums, most of which
are instrumental works. In 2017, he formed Call the Police, a band that
plays Police music (natch) and featured Andy and two Brazilian musicians.
Showing what a genius the man is, he was named Guitar Player of the Year
five different times in *Guitar Player* magazine and is now in the Hall of
Fame for that magazine.

Henry Padovani is still active in music as well. After his time with The
Police, Henry joined Wayne County & the Electric Chairs for a little while,
appearing on two albums and then formed the Flying Padovanis, who
released an EP and an album. Most people don't realize that Padovani was
named Vice President of I.R.S. Records by Miles Copeland, a role he had
from 1988 to 1994, and he also managed the hugely successful Italian singer/
songwriter Zucchero.

In 2007, Henry released a solo album that he sang in French called *À croire
que c'était pour la vie* and on that album, Sting and Stewart joined Padovani
on a song called 'Welcome Home' which was the first time the original Police
lineup had recorded in exactly 30 years (though they were not in the studio
at the same time for this recording). Also in 2007, Padovani released his
autobiography *Secret Police Man*.

In 2011, he was a judge on the French version of the *X Factor* and starred
in and produced a French rockumentary film called *Rock 'n' Roll... of Corse!*
with Sting, Stewart and Andy appearing, as well as Mick Jones and Topper
Headon of The Clash, Kim Wilde, Glen Matlock of the Sex Pistols and Jean-
Jacques Brunel of The Stranglers. The film is in both French and English
(and yes, the title is spelt the way it appears, I didn't spell it wrong). Henry
released a solo album called *I Love Today* in 2016 as well as a solo acoustic
live album in 2019.

The 1986 Amnesty International Concerts And Failed Studio Album

Regarding that 1986 Police activity, there was a good spirit and some optimism after the Amnesty International shows, because the band booked studio time for a new album that was to begin in July of 1986 with producer Laurie Latham, who had worked with Echo & Bunnymen, Ian Dury & the Blockheads, The Stranglers and Squeeze among others. To say the sessions went disastrously would be a major understatement. It became very obvious that Sting was calling all the shots and that the other guys had no choice but to follow if the band was to continue. Sting wanted to do an album of re-recordings which would be called *Every Breath You Take: The Songs*. Andy and Stewart were less than thrilled by the idea but figured once they got into the studio, the creative juices would start flowing, jams would occur and new material would develop – those plans went straight to hell.

Andy tells the tale in the liner notes on the *Message in a Box* set from 1993:

What can you say? That whole thing was absolutely torturous. The track is alright ('Don't Stand So Close to Me '86'), but the original's much better. This version took three weeks to record. I did my guitar part on the first night and the rest of the time it was Sting and Stewart arguing about whether the Fairlight or the Synclavier was better. The attempt to record a new album was doomed from the outset. The night before we went into the studio Stewart broke his collarbone falling off a horse and that meant we lost our last chance of recovering some rapport just by jamming together. Anyway, it was clear Sting had no real intention of writing any new songs for The Police. It was an empty exercise.

In 2007, as the reunion tour was starting rehearsals, Andy told *Rolling Stone* about this timeframe again: 'The studio was booked for three weeks. If Stewart hadn't fallen from his bloody horse, we would've jammed and out of that may have come something new'.

The song being referred to here is of course, 'Don't Stand So Close to Me '86', which will be discussed in a bit. One other song got to the demo stage and that was 'De Do Do Do, De Da Da Da '86', but it was not quite finished off, though it did see the light of day in 1995 and will also be discussed shortly.

Though there was never any grand statement or announcements, The Police were no more by the time *Every Breath You Take: The Singles* was released in October 1986. The album would sell over five million in the US, going quintuple-platinum and quadruple platinum in the UK, where it became their fifth straight album to hit number one. Sales were huge worldwide and yet they weren't even a band anymore.

There seemed to be virtually no hope of a reunion, although Summers appeared on two tracks from the Sting album *...Nothing Like the Sun* in 1987 and played three Police songs on stage with Sting and his band at the man's pay-per-view concert in Hollywood, CA on 2 October 1991 which was also Sting's birthday. When Sting married his new wife, Trudie Styler on 22 August 1992, Stewart and Andy were invited and were in attendance. The guys were coaxed by the wedding guests to play a few songs and obliged by playing 'Roxanne' and 'Message in a Bottle'. That same year, in 1992, *Greatest Hits* was issued and went double platinum in the UK, reaching the top ten and even quintuple platinum in Australia and platinum in other countries such as Canada, France and New Zealand.

Fans were thrilled with the previously mentioned four-disc box *Message in a Box: The Complete Recordings* released on 28 September 1993 that achieved platinum in the US (and gold in Canada) and, at the time, contained many rare items from throughout the career of the group. The vintage double-live album, imaginatively titled *Live!*, was put together and produced by Andy and featured two shows. One was from Boston, MA, on 27 November 1979 and the other from Atlanta, GA, on 2 November 1983.

In 2003, The Police were inducted into the *Rock and Roll Hall of Fame* and played 'Roxanne', 'Message in a Bottle' and 'Every Breath You Take' at the ceremony. On the latter song, they were pointlessly joined by Gwen Stefani of No Doubt, guitarist John Mayer and Steven Tyler of Aerosmith. Later that fall, Sting released his acclaimed book *Broken Music* to excellent reviews and delivered one of his very best solo tours.

On 12 December 2004, both Stewart and Andy joined eclectic hard alternative rockers Incubus on stage at the KROQ Almost Acoustic Christmas 2004 event at the Universal Amphitheater in Los Angeles, CA. They performed three Police songs together: 'De Do Do Do, De Da Da Da', 'Message in a Bottle' and 'Roxanne' – the crowd went bonkers. Vocalist Brandon Boyd is a very good singer in his own right, but struggled on some of the songs. Then again, who wouldn't? It was awesome seeing Stewart and Andy playing together again on a big stage and the crowd knew what they were seeing was quite special. Sting continued touring with a heavy accent on Police material with his excellent band.

Despite all this activity, Sting consistently stated that there would be no Police reunion tour and that he saw no reason to look backwards. He also added that he hadn't said the word 'never'.

The Reunion Era

In the history of rock and roll, there have been a few reunions that seemed literally impossible due to giant egos, financial squabbles, law suits, animosity, drugs, alcohol, and corrupt managers and so on.

Among the reunions that have occurred since the 1990s that seemed to have no chance in hell of happening were such bands as The Eagles (after all, they said hell would have to freeze over and jokingly named their 1994 reunion album as such), Steely Dan, Fleetwood Mac, The Who, the original lineup of Kiss, Journey, Styx, the original Black Sabbath and The Police to name a few. It seemed virtually impossible that any of these reunions could've occurred, and a Police reunion was at the top of the list.

The odds of a Police reunion shrank year by year, with Sting always saying: 'Why look back?' Well, in 2007, it finally happened on the band's 30th anniversary. Although the tour itself is covered in the Police tour section, this is how it came to pass. In the fall of 2006, Sting had been thinking about things differently following his forgettable album of lute music, *Songs from the Labyrinth*. He realized if the time was ever right, now was the time because he wasn't touring and he wasn't planning another solo album any time soon. He considered himself mad for considering a reunion but got over those issues and phone calls began. The Police secretly rehearsed in an informal setting at Sting's villa in Italy and things went well, both musically and socially.

Summers told *Mojo*: 'Sting's no virtuoso, but I go off into some weird place and he gets it; we both really feel it. Ah, we should have kept doing this. Something happens. It's undeniable'. Copeland added:

Those evenings were great. After 30 years, I hardly know Sting really. He's a sphinx. But to see him with Andy, the juices flowing, this torrent of visceral musicality, it's inspiring to hear that coming out of Sting, undisciplined, unthinking...

Sting offered his own thoughts:

It's true; we had very little in common in the beginning. What we share now is the band history. But we're not that close, though I do love 'em. I love them as brothers. And now I've done all the planning, all the cajoling, all the bullying I possibly can, I have learnt that my pursuit of perfection is the right way to go, but...I'm not really interested in that result anymore.

Sting also told *Rolling Stone* as the band was starting rehearsals:

I couldn't do this if it was just for the money. It's about me having a good time and hearing the music develop. That makes me happy. I want them to enjoy it, too. But they can't enjoy it unless I'm having a good time.

He went on to say: 'I'm doing this for myself. I really am'.

Sting told the interviewer that in November of 2006, he asked himself, 'What the fuck do I do now?' He was referring to having just released his album of lute music and had no touring or recording plans at that time. He told the magazine: 'What clinched it, was thinking, 'What would surprise people? What would surprise me?' 'Surprise is everything'. He added: 'It certainly surprised the guys'.

Copeland said in the same article:

Sting is a recording artist who has to plot his course very carefully. For him to take twenty steps back like this, it's a career move and the reason he can call me with the expectation that my answer will be an immediate yes.

As for their takes on the tour, Sting said: 'I'm not claiming infallibility. I just had a feeling this would be the right time. The hoopla and the ticket sales prove that. It's the *perfect* time'. Copeland said:

I'm not going to change my life at all as a result of this tour. I live a very simple life. I drive a Jeep Cherokee and have one house. And if you subtract the money, this is a still a good idea. You get to play to crowds that will go nuts and tour the world with songs that everybody loves.

As for Andy, he stated:

No, don't need the money. It's nice to get it. We've got into that lovely top drawer where our records were essential for a certain generation. We left this energy, this mythology. Maybe it's because we stopped before we blew it.

Sting's last words for the interview were accurate:

There is a maturity in all of us, even though the energy between us is kind of puppyish. We have all raised families, maintained marriages, and maintained careers. It has given us resilience and some blisters. I like them (Stewart and Andy). I like them more.

He went on: 'But it's an interesting position to put us in, a little Petri dish. It's different from the way it was twenty, thirty years ago. We are able to navigate better. Stay friends'. He concluded with a laugh: 'I hope. There's no guarantee, though'.

And with that, they embarked on the magical reunion tour that shattered box office records and offered ample evidence that this band were still a musical force.

Looking back years later, in March 2021, Sting talked about the reunion tour and told *Reader's Digest*: 'At the time, I labelled the tour an exercise in nostalgia. That was simply how I felt and is still how I feel today. I think it's OK to be honest about your feelings and that was the way it went for me'. He added:

That's not a slight on the people I was with or the way things panned out, it's just how I saw it by the end, and let's be honest, that's not how I wanted to remember it. If I thought that would be the emotion I'd be leaving with, I wouldn't have done it in the first place. It's not a power thing at all; it's just about producing exactly the brand and style of music that feels right for you. Music, in every form, is a collaborative process, but never more so than in a band, where you have to consider other people almost more than you do yourself.

Copeland also discussed the tour in 2019 and said there was no need for another reunion:

Right now, it's just so great to hang with my buddies, who are like brothers, without clouding it with the issue. The issue is that although we're very proud of the music we made and very proud of the impact of the band, it was very difficult. The music each of us makes in our own world now is very wonderful and rewarding. We know that when we go in that rehearsal room together, we're going to start screaming at each other again, and I'd rather laugh.

Coda. Summers V Sting?

In October 2023, Andy Summers revealed to listeners of *The Jeremy White Show* that he was in a contentious battle with Sting over songwriting credits for 'Every Breath You Take', hinting at possible legal action. Summers said:

> 'Every Breath You Take' was going in the trash until I played on it. It's a very contentious [topic] – it's very much alive at the moment. Watch the press; let's see what happens in the next year.

While at the time of writing in early 2024, any legal action was yet to emerge, it's interesting that even 40 years on, issues like this – with its parallels to Matthew Fisher's lawsuit for a credit to 'A Whiter Shade Of Pale', where the musician won rights to royalties for his famed organ part – how the moral and legal rights to a song can still be in dispute.

Watch this space. The Police story isn't over yet.

The Police Compilation Albums

Every Breath You Take: The Singles (1986)

Highest chart position: UK: 1, US: 7, Canada: 11, Germany: 18, Australia: 4, France: 1

The studio album of re-recordings was abandoned, leading to this: the first compilation album of music from The Police. Issued in October of 1986, the album became a colossal seller even though the group was essentially over by that point, although nothing official about a breakup was ever actually announced.

This album would become the band's fifth straight number one album in the UK and also peaked at number seven in the US. Sales were through the roof as the album achieved quadruple platinum in the UK, quintuple platinum in the US, platinum in Canada and New Zealand and double platinum in France. The album would spend just shy of a solid year on the album charts in the UK for 51 weeks straight.

The CD had one additional track that the vinyl did not, which was 'So Lonely'. Other classics included were 'Roxanne', 'Can't Stand Losing You', 'Message in a Bottle', 'Walking on the Moon', 'De Do Do Do, De Da Da Da', 'Every Little Thing She Does is Magic', 'Invisible Sun', 'Spirits in the Material World', 'Every Breath You Take', 'King of Pain' and 'Wrapped Around Your Finger'. The brand new recording 'Don't Stand So Close to Me '86' was also included and was a major selling point. So, this album amounted to the band's farewell.

In 1995, the album was reissued as *Every Breath You Take: The Classics* and contained a slightly expanded track listing by adding the original 'Don't Stand So Close to Me' (the 1986 version stayed as well) and a new remix of another track 'Message in a Bottle' (dubbed the 'Classic Rock Mix'). The bigger news was the further reissue of this for a DTS (Digital Theater System) release in 2000 and once more for a hybrid SACD (Super Audio CD) in 2003. These versions included the unreleased 'De Do Do Do, De Da Da Da '86' which to this day still appears on no other Police compilations.

'Don't Stand So Close to Me '86' (Sting)

In those liner notes on the *Message in a Box* collection, Stewart Copeland offered up his version of what happened with this recording in typically hilarious fashion:

> Well, my horse did a forward somersault and I was forced to dismount. I was entirely venomless, sedated as I was by painkillers, but I managed (accidentally, I swear!) to fatally insult Sting. We exchanged long, mutually abusive letters and took turns in the studio recording over each other's parts. Finally, after wasting several weeks, Miles said, 'Look, children, you will both have to share the same room to mix this track'. I had no problem with this (it was Sting who stormed out) and was there for the mix at 10 o'clock sharp. We proceeded to mix, while waiting all day for word of our esteemed

leader. I was just getting hrumphy and beginning to make speeches when Sting showed up with a rose, a hug and a 12-inch switchblade.

In an interview with *Mojo* magazine in 2007 during the reunion tour, Stewart also added to that knife incident when he recalled this anecdote: 'Sting said, 'This (the knife) is for you, Copeland!' We got along famously for the rest of the day and the snare drum on that single is a mix of the two samples'.

This version of the song is actually pretty good and well-conceived. There's a feel of melancholy and the moodiness of the keyboard and guitar synth chords are excellent accents that change the song. The end result is very downbeat and dark. Sting's bass is very prominent and Andy plays some nifty parts that are very different from the original. The programmed drums are clattery and mechanized sounding, a combo of the Fairlight and the Synclavier that caused so much agony.

The backing vocals are well done and the fade also works well where you can hear Sting go into some higher registers in the backing voices that come up in the mix. The lyrics take on a darker meaning in this version, though none of them are altered from the original, with the exception of the change from 'Just like the old man in that book by Nabokov' to adding 'famous' before the word book. All in all, this was a pretty good re-working of a classic song. There's a cool acapella vocal part towards the end that brings the song to a stop and the drums kick in towards the fade. Not every fan was on board, and some hated it, but the song performed admirably, reaching number 25 in the UK and number 46 in the US, as well as number 27 in Canada. It topped the charts in Spain, also reaching the top twenty in The Netherlands, Finland, New Zealand and Ireland, where it stopped just shy of the top ten. The song also peaked at number ten on Album Rock in the US and received substantial play on MTV. While the re-recording wasn't close to vintage Police, it was different, more than an acceptable attempt at creating something new with something old.

As for the music video, Godley and Creme did their best as the band members couldn't be in the same room together, so a lot of editing and digitizing took place. Cutting-edge computer graphics were used and the video was colourful, utilizing the primary colours from *Synchronicity* quite cleverly. Vintage clips are included, as well as current shots of the guys looking like some sort of evil cult slowly spinning in circles.

The twelve-inch dance mix runs six and a half minutes and has some neat features, including a ticking clock and floating synth parts. Andy also rips off a wicked guitar solo, which only appears on this version, which has only surfaced on CD on the German version of *Message in a Box* in 1993. Besides appearing on *Every Breath You Take: The Singles*, 'Don't Stand So Close to Me '86' also shows up on *Every Breath You Take: The Classics* and closes the US version of the *Message in a Box* release from 1993. The UK release of that box set did not have either version.

'De Do Do Do, De Da Da Da '86' (Sting)

This re-recording came from the 1986 sessions and was never released until being included on the 1995 compilation album *Every Breath You Take: The Classics*, but only appeared on the DTS and SACD issues of that release in 2000 and 2003, respectively.

This version is similar to what one would imagine Sting doing in his solo career. It's very adult contemporary, saccharine and not very imaginative. It is bright and sunny, but it lacks any of the charm of the original. The vocals are the strongest point as the instrumentation is let down by some blasé bass lines and guitar parts and stiff drum programming. Even the bridge is rather weak here.

Allegedly, this is a Sting solo demo that he presented to the band before the recording sessions. Indeed, it doesn't sound like Summers and Copeland had much, if any impact on this version, but it's hard to tell completely if they weren't part of the recording. It most definitely sounds like a demo, though, not in a rough sense but more in an unfinished sense. It's very unlikely Andy and Stewart had a thing to do with this recording and had this arrangement been properly finished off, it still wouldn't have been a good idea.

This track was not included on either box set or, for that matter, any other Police compilation other than the two versions of *Every Breath You Take: The Classics* mentioned above.

'Message In A Bottle' (New Classic Rock Mix) (Sting)

This new remix appeared on the *Every Breath You Take: The Classics* compilation and is hardly any different from the original, with a slight emphasis on the rhythm guitars and vocals, the keyboards lower in the mix and the bass largely unchanged. Was there any real need for this mix? No, and it's not really radically different or creative enough to make it worthwhile. I'm not sure what the point of this even was. Nobody is credited for the mix, but it may have been Phil Nicolo, as a CD-R acetate in the UK from 1995 had this mix listed as the 'Phil Nicolo '95 Remix' and that appears to be the version that is here.

Greatest Hits (1992)

Highest chart position: UK: 10, Canada: 24, Germany: 18, Australia: 16, France: 1
The marketing department of A&M Records clearly spent months coming up with a name for this collection. This is a more expansive collection than the first compilation from 1986, as it includes sixteen tracks. The additions here to the previous collection are 'The Bed's Too Big Without You', 'Synchronicity II' and 'Tea in the Sahara'.

This collection hit number ten in the UK as well as the top spot in France and New Zealand and would also reach number 24 in Canada, and the top twenty in Germany and Australia. It was barely promoted in the US and failed to chart there. Double platinum status was obtained in the UK, quintuple platinum in Australia, and platinum in Canada, France and New Zealand.

The cover photograph was from the *Synchronicity* era and was shot by Duane Michals. A collage of photos was used on the interior booklet, with photos shot by a variety of people, including both Miles Copeland and Andy Summers. The album would chart for a hefty 36 weeks in the UK.

The Very Best Of ... Sting & The Police (1997)

Highest chart position: UK: 1, US: 46, Canada: 66, Germany: 18, Australia: 22, France: 1

This compilation tried to combine both Sting and Police tracks into one package, but there simply wasn't enough space to justify such a thing on one CD. The collection is out of sequence and haphazardly has Sting and Police songs in no particular order.

The one 'bonus' selection here was 'Roxanne '97', which was a remix of the old gem from 1978 by none other than Puff Daddy. The collection went to number one in the UK somehow and also hit number 46 in the US, where it went gold. Top ten positions were achieved in France, Belgium, Finland, New Zealand, Austria, Ireland, Italy and Denmark.

There were several reissues with different track listings in 1998 and again in 2002 (this version is the one that topped the UK charts). Quadruple platinum was achieved in the UK and double platinum in France, with platinum in Argentina. Gold status was scored in Australia, Austria, Germany, Italy, Japan, New Zealand, Spain, and Switzerland.

'Roxanne '97 (The Puff Daddy Mix)' (Campbell/Fequiere/Full Force/ Sting)

This remix was handled by Puff Daddy (aka Sean Combs) in 1997 for the compilation album mentioned above. It is officially credited to Sting & The Police Featuring Pras and starred the group Full Force on backing vocals. Songs that were sampled include the UTFO song 'Roxanne, Roxanne', Kool & The Gang's 'Kool's Back Again', snippets of James Brown's 'Blind Man Can See It' and 'Bouncy Lady' by Pleasure.

The mix has...mixed results. The marriage of hip-hop and rock had happened long ago, but sometimes artists hopped on board for 'street cred' for some unknown reason: Paul McCartney and Kanye West, anyone? Anyway, this isn't entirely bad, saved by some effective sampling choices and Sting's slowed-down vocals, which make the song more dramatic. The production is impressive, but things quickly become fairly dull. Once you're past the first chorus, it's an endurance test and the quotes from the UTFO song become ingratiating.

Pras did the rap vocals, with Full Force providing the backing vocals. Pras was a member of The Fugees, whose real name is Prakazrel Samuel Michel. The Fugees also included Wyclef Jean and Lauryn Hill and were quite popular and successful in the late 1990s. Issued as a single in December 1997, the remix would reach number 59 on the US charts and spent thirteen weeks on the listings. If you've never heard it, you're not missing much, but if you're curious, it could've been worse.

The Police (2007)

Highest chart position: UK: 3, US: 11, Germany: 78, Australia: 17, France: 2
By far the best Police compilation out there, this double best-of was issued on 5 June 2007 to tie in with the start of the enormously successful reunion tour of 2007-08. Most versions featured 28 tracks, but some versions, like the one released in the UK, offered up 30 songs.

The track listing is in chronological order and the mastering comes from the Bob Ludwig remasters of the five studio albums from 2003, therefore all feature excellent sound. Two semi-rare items are on the set, most surprising being 'Fall Out', which was the band's debut single from 1977, celebrating its 30th anniversary that year. This was a very cool inclusion and a great way to start things off as many people who bought this collection probably didn't even know of 'Fall Out' or that it featured Henry Padovani and not Andy Summers on guitar. The other mild surprise is 'Murder by Numbers', which was from 1983 and had only appeared on the cassette and early CD versions of *Synchronicity* but was also a B-side. Of course, by this point, it had already appeared on the remastered version of the album and the box set. It's not rare at all, but it's a nice inclusion.

There are six tracks from *Outlandos d'Amour*, four from *Regatta de Blanc*, five from *Zenyatta Mondatta*, five from *Ghost in the Machine* and from *Synchronicity,* there are a whopping total of eight tracks (including 'Murder by Numbers') and of course, there's also 'Fall Out'. The two extra tracks that appeared on the international editions were 'The Bed's Too Big Without You' and 'Rehumanize Yourself'.

The album hit number three in the UK and number eleven in the US, showing just how beloved this band's songs still were. This collection also went platinum in the UK, double platinum in Ireland, and gold in Canada, Belgium and New Zealand. The comp went top ten in Belgium, Denmark, The Netherlands, Ireland, New Zealand and Norway. Not too shabby from a band that hadn't recorded anything new since 1986!

The Police Live Albums

Live! (1995)

Highest chart position: UK: 25, US: 86, Canada: 57, Germany: 43, France: 4

Once again, A&M got their crack research and marketing team to come up with a name for the first-ever live album from The Police. It took hours and hours of brainstorming and we got...*Live!* All kidding aside, it was very cool to have an official live document from The Police, even if it was nearly a decade after they had disbanded. The release was a two-CD set that featured a live show from Boston, MA, in 1979 on disc one and a live show from Atlanta, GA, in 1983 on disc two.

A live album had been mooted by the band as far back as 1982 and it was even mastered in Montreal, Quebec, Canada at Le Studio but was scrapped and never released (why we didn't get that album here, who knows?). Another live album was being prepared for release for the Christmas season of 1984 and some FM radio stations in the US leaked tracks from it, but this too never surfaced (although most of that is on disc two of this release).

The idea was revived in the mid-1990s and Andy Summers oversaw the release of *Live!* which was issued on 29 May 1995. The show in Boston was recorded at the Orpheum Theatre on 27 November 1979 and was originally a radio broadcast on popular Boston rock station WBCN-FM. The concert features tracks from the first two LPs as well as non-album songs such as 'Landlord' and 'Fall Out', which show the band's punk phase was still intact.

Tracks that would eventually stop getting live performances were played as well, such as 'Peanuts', 'The Bed's Too Big Without You' and 'Be My Girl-Sally'. It is not the complete show, however, as 'Deathwish' and 'Visions of the Night' were excised, which is a shame, but this was done for the practical purpose of fitting the concert onto one disc. The quality of the show is very good, although many fans already had the recording as a bootleg from the initial FM broadcast or the numerous rebroadcasts of the show in later years. This is a very nice live document of the band in their earlier years and they rock it out.

The second disc is from the stand in Atlanta, GA, on 2 and 3 November 1983 that were also used for the hugely popular concert video *Synchronicity Concert* (another amazing title...how do they do it?) from 1984. This disc features the band very polished, professional and tight but still maintaining the excitement of the old days with just a little less chaotic.

Again, this is far from a complete show as many songs performed are missing and those are: 'Walking on the Moon', 'Hole in My Life' 'Invisible Sun', 'One World (Not Three)' and 'Murder by Numbers'. Had we received these concerts as separate releases, we could've had double CD sets for each and received the entire shows, but they made the choice to go down the route of one disc for each show; thus, some songs had to go.

The quality is fantastic here and there are lots of reasons to still love this release, even with the absent tracks. The 1983 show is also augmented with backing vocals from Dolette McDonald, Tessa Niles and Michelle Cobb. This show also sees the band stretching out musically and veering from the album arrangements, which is what they expounded upon on the reunion tour.

Live! would reach number 86 on the US charts and impressively went platinum, selling over one million copies. In the UK, the album hit number 25 and a live version of 'Can't Stand Losing You' from the 1979 show was released as a single and peaked at number 27 in late 1995. To date, this is the only Police standalone live album, although a double CD was included in the DVD and Blu-Ray release of *Certifiable: Live in Buenos Aires* in 2008.

For Record Store Day on 12 June 2021, each concert was issued on vinyl as *Live Vol. 1 Boston 1979* and *Live Vol. 2 Atlanta 1983,* with these particular releases being the first time that the recordings had ever been issued on vinyl, as vinyl was almost non-existent back when *Live!* originally came out in 1995. The Boston LP is etched in blue vinyl and the Atlanta LP in red vinyl. Unfortunately, there are no extra tracks added, even though songs were missing from each concert.

The Police Box Sets

Six Pack (1980)

Highest chart position: UK: 17

Released to capitalize on the band's surging popularity, this boxset packaged six singles which were 'Roxanne', 'Can't Stand Losing You', 'So Lonely', 'Message in a Bottle', 'Walking on the Moon' and a mono version of 'The Bed's Too Big Without You' which differed from the original recording as discussed earlier.

Each single was on blue vinyl and included special picture cards of the band members with three solo shots and three group shots. The lyrics from each single were also printed on the back. The mono version of 'The Bed's Too Big Without You' would surface on the 1993 box set. Qualifying as a single release, this would reach number 17 on the UK charts in June 1980.

Message In A Box: The Complete Recordings (1993)

Highest chart position: US: 79

One of the best boxsets in existence, this four-disc collection released on 28 September 1993 contained all five studio albums and a litany of B-sides, live tracks and rarities. This collection does exactly what a boxset is supposed to; it gives the casual and the diehard fan reason to purchase it and is an effective career-encompassing retrospective.

The rare tracks were very hard to find at the time and many had never been on CD or an official release before. There were some live tracks that were B-sides as well as some live tracks from compilation albums of various artists. For example, explosive takes on both 'Landlord' and 'Next to You' were recorded at the Bottom Line in New York on 4 April 1979 and had only appeared on the compilation album *Propaganda-No Wave II*, while a live version of 'Driven to Tears', from the awesome 1982 concert film *Urgh! A Music War*, was included (the soundtrack actually appeared in 1981 before the film was released in theatres the following year).

The box also includes all three Police songs from the *Brimstone & Treacle* soundtrack from 1982 and live B-sides of 'Man in a Suitcase', 'Message in a Bottle' and 'Tea in the Sahara' from 1983. A few other live B-sides are missing, though, including 'Wrapped Around Your Finger' and 'Don't Stand So Close to Me'. Both rare tracks from the *Six Pack* release are included and every B-side previously covered for the individual albums above are here as well.

The box set opens with 'Fall Out' and closes with 'Don't Stand So Close to Me '86'. This fully sums up quite a career. The German version of the box ends not with the known version of 'Don't Stand So Close to Me '86', but the rare 12-inch dance mix has appeared nowhere else but on that German version of the box. Also absent from this box are any rare demos, and the two foreign language versions of 'De Do Do Do, De Da Da Da' as well as 'De Do Do Do, De Da Da Da '86'.

The packaging, the photos, the interviews, the track commentary and the mastering by Dave Collins are all excellent. The box earned instant critical praise and was coveted by fans around the world. It also sold incredibly well for a box set, going platinum in the US and gold in Canada, which was highly unusual. Bravo to everyone involved.

Every Move You Make: The Studio Recordings (2018)
Highest chart position: UK: 17

Initially, a vinyl-only UK release in 2018, this boxset came to CD, issued worldwide on 15 November 2019 and was a revelation. Included were all five studio albums newly remastered for the first time since 2003 and a sixth disc of rare tracks called *Flexible Strategies*. Each individual album was in a mini-cardboard sleeve packaging with a gatefold replica and looked great.

Sadly, no booklet was included with any liner notes, but the music is what matters here and the oversized clamshell case the discs came in, containing a blue ribbon that held the albums to protect them, was a very nice compliment. Care went into this release and the mastering was mostly excellent. One noticeable difference is that the drums are louder, but they don't sound overly compressed.

One can easily turn these up with enjoyment and not worry about any screeching sounds or ear-bleeding. The listener is also going to notice how much more punch there is with the bass and bottom end, as well as more prominence for the guitars and keyboards. I personally liked the Bob Ludwig remasters from 2003, but some fans and audiophiles did not for whatever reason. However, these new remasters are radically different and really do sound fuller. Myles Showall at Abbey Road Studios did the mastering for the vinyl and it's reasonable to assume the CDs were transferred from the vinyl of his work.

Very reasonably priced, the boxset sold well, still sells well and even made the UK top twenty. If you're a fan, this box set is a great way of having everything in one place with excellent sound and packaging. As for those deluxe editions of the individual albums Stewart talked about a few years ago, those have not surfaced or even been discussed as of this book's printing.

Flexible Strategies (2018)

This disc was the sixth in the boxset and was named after a Police B-side from 1981. It was a very nice collection of Police rarities, but all save one had appeared on *Message in a Box* back in 1993. These are newly remastered and, for the most part, sound very good, although one or two songs seem to have been sourced from second or third-generation copies of the masters, not that that's a bad thing – you are still getting them in very good quality.

Two things of note here: The 1981 B-side 'Shambelle' had its first three seconds missing on the 1993 box set, but they have been properly restored here, which almost certainly means this is from the original master tape. Also, one inclusion that had never been on a Police album release is here with 'Truth Hits Everybody', which is listed as a remix but is actually a re-recording from 1983 that was on a UK-only 7-inch gatefold single of 'Every Breath You Take'. It's an excellent version and its inclusion here is a delight.

The twelve tracks selected here are as follows: 'Dead End Job', 'Landlord', 'Visions of the Night', 'Friends', 'A Sermon', 'Shambelle', 'Flexible Strategies', 'Low Life', 'Murder by Numbers', 'Truth Hits Everybody (remix)', 'Someone to Talk To' and 'Once Upon a Daydream'. The disc clocks in at around 43 minutes and since it was first done for vinyl, the running time is shorter than one would hope. That being said, as nice as the box is, most fans had virtually all of this material already. The CD obviously could've been loaded up with more rare tracks.

If you take out the live B-sides, a number of others should've made the cut here. The 1977 debut single 'Fall Out' and its B-side, 'Nothing Achieving' are no-brainers. The three cuts from the 1982 film soundtrack of *Brimstone & Treacle* were also obvious choices to include as well as 'Don't Stand So Close to Me '86' (both the album version and the rare 12-inch mix), 'De Do Do Do, De Da Da Da '86' and the two foreign language versions of 'De Do Do Do, De Da Da Da'. It was a missed opportunity for sure, but no real complaints should be lodged. This box was an unexpected surprise for fans and the presentation and sonic quality is top-notch. Now, let's get those deluxe editions of the albums with vintage live shows and bonus tracks out there soon.

'Truth Hits Everybody' (remix) (Sting)

Recorded during the album sessions for *Synchronicity*, this is closer to a re-recording than a remix of the song, originally appearing on the 1978 debut album *Outlandos d'Amour*. The arrangements are downbeat and the song sounds much more introspective and mellow.

The changes work incredibly well even though the song doesn't much resemble the original, save for the chorus. The idea for an album of re-recordings was obviously something Sting had been thinking about for a while. Some elements of this arrangement were used on the reunion tour. It's likely that this rearrangement would've been utilized for the new album in 1986, though they likely would've polished it off more.

This version also sounds very 'of the moment' and was probably recorded in one take. At times, Sting seems to be mostly mumbling the melody and only occasionally offering a clear vocal. The drums sound like they are a smaller practice kit and certainly not Stewart's classic Tama setup. The live, demo feel is very neat to hear in this capacity. This recording never appeared on an album until being included on the 2019 box set.

Strontium 90 Albums

Strontium 90: Police Academy (1997)

Personnel:

Mike Howlett: lead bass, lead and backing vocals

Sting: bass, lead and backing vocals, acoustic guitar and African drum on 'Every Little Thing She Does is Magic'

Andy Summers: guitars

Stewart Copeland: drums, percussion

Released: 29 July 1997 (recorded 1977)

Recorded: Virtual Earth Studio in London, UK; Cirque Hippodrome in Paris, France

Produced by: Mike Howlett

Engineer: Joe Julian

Cover Design: Emilie Burnham

For the uninitiated, this was a history lesson as to where the classic Police lineup originated. As mentioned earlier, Strontium 90 was quickly put together by Mike Howlett for a Gong reunion show in Paris, France, on 28 May 1977. It was here where Sting and Stewart first met and played with Andy Summers. Thankfully, someone had the forethought to record the proceedings as well as the studio sessions that took place. Twenty years later, in 1997, what was still in the archives was put together for this release.

The quality isn't audiophile for the live tracks, but it was way better than anyone could've expected and it's definitely not a bootleg or unauthorized release. The studio tracks included a few gems that were fairly well recorded demos, especially the rocking 'New World Blues', which has some great hooks, riffs and excellent lead. Dare I say this is as good as any early Police song? This is music worth repeated listens and shows how good the guys were, even having barely played together at this point.

Howlett's voice is good on the tracks that he sings on and he's an excellent bass player; it's a little odd hearing two bass players, but Howlett goes high up the neck for some 'lead bass' at times and Sting keeps the bottom end going. Stewart and Andy are both up to the task and rock out quite nicely, showcasing their chops.

Police fans will notice there's a Sting solo demo of 'Every Little Thing She Does is Magic' and an early version of 'Visions of the Night', which would be a staple of early live shows for the band and would be reworked for a Police B-side. Also, the rocker '3 O'Clock Shot' (it's actually called '3 O'Clock Shit') has as its main riff the one that became 'Be My Girl-Sally' on *Outlands d'Amour,* and there are lyrics that would later appear on 'O My God' from *Synchronicity* as well as a hanging chord that would be used on 'Hole in My Life' from the debut album.

The tracks range from punk and early new wave to funk and alternative music. The dual bass playing actually stands out quite a bit and isn't a distraction at all. Sting and Howlett sing really well together. The drums are blocky sounding, but you can clearly hear he had the chops, having already played with Curved Air.

The songs were put together quickly and more development would've helped on a few tracks, but a lot of this is really choice material. It's great that this material got an official release, although it wasn't hyped all that much and came out on an indie label (Pangaea/Ark 21 Records), consequently failing to make the charts. Had more people been made aware of it and actually known what exactly this material was, it could've sold better.

If you've never heard it, it's worth your while and a really neat time capsule showcasing Sting, Stewart and Andy just before their deserved rise to superstardom.

'Visions Of The Night' (Sting)

This hyper-charged punk rocker isn't too dissimilar at all from the version that The Police ultimately recorded. The melody and guitar lines are basically the same, as is the structure of the song. Sting sings in a very high register and there's a harmony vocal which sounds like Sting, but Howlett is also in there somewhere.

What we're hearing is a rougher recording of the song that The Police would use to record the B-side a few years later. The drums aren't mixed all that well and are fairly straightforward, but Stewart gets a few fills in the intro. The lyrics are the same as what would end up on The Police recording, which is the superior version of the two.

'New World Blues' (Howlett)

After a mysterious hanging guitar chord, the main riff explodes with energy and hooks and flat-out rocks. The bass (both of them) and the guitars are interlocked in a tight, insistent riff and Stewart is on the money with fills and cymbals galore. Howlett sounds outstanding vocally and Andy has some truly tasty solos that pierce the song and are very thematic and memorable. This song sounds tailor-made for FM rock radio. It sure sounds like Sting drops in an 'F-bomb' in excitement at one point.

'3 O'Clock Shot' (Live) (Sting)

Incorrectly listed as '3 O'Clock Shot' when its real name was the less-charming '3 O'Clock Shit', this was another song that would survive into the world of early Police material.

The opening muted guitar riff is clearly the one that The Police would use as the main riff in 'Be My Girl-Sally' on *Outlandos d'Amour* and some of these lyrics would be recycled for use on 'O My God' from 1983's *Synchronicity* album. The bass playing is very bubbly and prominent here and Stewart drums with abandon when he has a chance to add fills.

This was one of the tracks recorded at the Gong gig on 28 May 1977 in Paris, France. Though a bit muffled and with not enough treble, the recording is generally fine, with everything mostly audible. The song is rather repetitive until the 3:30 mark when a hanging chord, like that would be used on 'Hole in My Life' (also from the debut Police album), hits and then Sting quietly moans away for a bit before the main riff comes back in.

Running over five minutes long, this one becomes a bit tiresome, but it's definitely exciting hearing the early sounds that The Police would later use. The song's original title was 'Love is in My Heart' and Stewart told Sting to change it to '3 O'Clock Shit' to sound more punk.

'Lady Of Delight' (Howlett)
Here's another song that flat-out rocks with plenty of hooks and attitude. Howlett nails it vocally and Sting comes in on the bridge, leading to a snarling slide guitar solo from Summers as Stewart flashes and bashes with class and finesse. The song is catchy, to the point and filled with spirit and vivacious playing. Howlett's background would've led you to expect a lot of weirdness and psychedelic touches, but instead, we get a tight batch of memorable rockers with expert playing and great hooks.

Songs like this were ready for FM rock radio in the late 1970s and it's a shame nobody really heard them until twenty years after the fact.

'Electron Romance' (Howlett)
Although the title might lead one to think this was an Ultravox or Gary Numan-styled song, it's quite the opposite. The song is irresistibly funky, with fat bass grooves from both Howlett and Sting alongside punchy guitars by Andy.

Howlett and Sting both sing lead vocals on this one and Stewart gets his groove on. A change to double time livens things up in a different direction while the bass bubbles all over the place. It sounds like Howlett is playing a fretless, particularly when he plays lead bass. The song does lose some steam when it veers from the funk into the quicker pace, but only because the groove that they were locked into was so satisfying.

However, the funk comes back and Stewart mixes in hi-hat and ride cymbal to change dynamics. The song eventually stops on a dime.

'Every Little Thing She Does Is Magic' (demo) (Sting)
This beautiful solo demo of the future Police classic captures Sting in an intimate setting way back around 1977 or so when he was still writing songs with no real idea of where they would end up.

It's just Sting on strummed acoustic guitar, bass guitar, vocals and a bit of an African drum for percussion. The basic framework of the song is here already, with a few melodic differences. The lyrics are the same and it's hard to fathom that this masterpiece sat in the vaults for five years before The Police recorded it in 1981 for *Ghost in the Machine*, where it became the first single and a worldwide smash. Sting's voice has excellent sustain and control even at this juncture and his writing is fantastic.

Mike Howlett recorded this, capturing Sting on a TEAC four-track tape recorder in his attic studio in Chiswick, a suburb of London. Sting had recently written the song and wanted to lay it down on tape so he could remember the chords, melody and feel. It's a great thing that happened for many reasons, obviously, but this version is simply lovely.

'Towers Tumbled' (Howlett)

This song has an alternative rock feel that has similar qualities to the sounds that Talking Heads, XTC and others were starting to use at the same time. Howlett's vocals sound similar to Greg Lake in his King Crimson days, the song has an odd rhythm and structure, and Summers gets in some more slide licks that add to the mood.

This song bears no resemblance to The Police at all, where some of the others, you can hear musical styles they utilized later. There's lots of lead bass again, which you either dig or find obtrusive. One thing about this song is that it doesn't deviate much at all from the opening ideas, so what you hear is what you get right from the start.

Tacked onto the Strontium 90 album were live versions of 'Electron Romance' and 'Lady of Delight' and the Japanese 2011 remaster added two more live cuts with performances of the song 'New World Blues' as well as 'Towers Tumbled'.

Howlett would go on to produce quite a few names in the music industry, including A Flock of Seagulls, The Alarm, Orchestral Manoeuvers in the Dark, Gang of Four, Tears for Fears, Blancmange and Berlin. He also still participates in Gong reunion shows and received a PhD in record production in 2009, often lecturing at universities. He also became Head of Music at Queensland University of Technology in Brisbane, Australia.

The Police Video Releases

Under Miles Copeland, it's no surprise that The Police took advantage of the music video medium because Miles was always thinking forward and using more ways than one to market and promote the band at any chance he got.

There were a number of Police releases on home video and some of those haven't even seen the light of day on DVD or Blu-Ray and still languish on the antiquated VHS or even Betamax formats. There are only two true official live concerts of the band on video, but there are also some great professionally shot shows that are out there that were never officially released.

This section only takes a brief look at the significant releases that hit the marketplace and were released in various video formats between 1982 and 2013.

Police Around The World (1982)

This was easily one of the best home video releases in music of its kind. The combination of documentary/interview/performance footage can sometimes be an annoyance and most fans usually just want a full-on concert video. However, this release really came out great as it shows the band on their bizarre tour of 1980-81 playing unusual locales at the time, such as India, Egypt, Greece and Singapore, to name a few. The images of the band arriving in Japan are amusing and Andy gets to tangle with a sumo wrestler, which is one of many ridiculous scenes in the film which make it a great watch.

Concert footage of the band is interspersed throughout and was shot in Frejus, France, on 28 August 1980 and looks great shot in film, although the audio is way too high in treble and there's very little bottom end. During a performance of 'De Do Do Do, De Da Da Da', Sting becomes understandably irate, shouting profanities as some loser decided to gob at him. Security did get the fool, but that isn't shown.

In India, we see the guys jamming on tabla drums, sitar and upright bass. Sting also sees a snake charmer on the street and witnesses an unpleasant mongoose versus snake fight that doesn't end well for the mongoose. There's a really nice part where we meet the Indian ladies who promoted and organized the concert, and they almost faint at a shirtless Sting.

In Egypt, there is much drama as the band's equipment is held up in customs, which leads to an awesome argument between Miles and Ian Copeland while Ian is on a camel in front of the pyramids. Stewart is also involved and everyone nearly comes to blows – this is classic stuff. Rights issues have held up the release of this on DVD or Blu-Ray, but it needs to be issued in those formats one day.

Urgh! A Music War (1982)

Hands down, this was one of the very best concert documentaries of all-time. Released in May 1982 in theaters for a brief run, the humorously titled *Urgh! A Music War* captured well over 30 different musical acts – mostly from new wave and punk circles – live in concert and shot on film directed by Derek Burbidge, who also directed the *Police Around the World* video.

Most of the acts were filmed in various locales in the US and UK, whilst some bands shot in Frejus, France. The acts selected were an amazing mix of the crème de la crème of the genre, such as Echo & Bunnymen, XTC, Oingo Boingo, Dead Kennedys, Gary Numan, Devo, Klaus Nomi, Magazine, X, The Go-Go's, Joan Jett and the Blackhearts, Wall of Voodoo, Gang of Four and loads more including a few obscure acts.

Miles Copeland owned the film rights and his clients – The Police – appear here with three songs. All the other acts only have one song, although the zany Klaus Nomi gets multiple looks as he gets a second song played over the end credits.

The Police open the film with a fantastic version of 'Driven to Tears' and conclude the documentary with renditions of 'Roxanne' and 'So Lonely'. A double-live album had preceded the film's release in 1981, but only 'Driven to Tears' appears on the album and a number of other acts are absent from the vinyl.

This film first hit the home video market in 1985 and was a Videodisc release, though that format eventually died out and the film was out of print for years. In the US, the documentary got a fair amount of showings on the USA Network late at night on weekends and developed a cult following. Finally, in 2009, all of the red tape involved with defunct studios and various record labels allowed the full, original film to hit DVD for the first time when Warner Archives gave it a release on-demand. Although the film is not remastered, it looks and sounds excellent and is presented in widescreen.

The music does all the talking here, as there's no backstage footage, interviews or superfluous material. You get a ton of acts and a ton of music and it delivers in a big way. Obviously, The Police were the big draw here, but the multitude of different acts is also a huge grabbing point and this film really is an absolute must for any music fan, especially of new wave and punk rock.

Synchronicity Concert (1984)

This Godley & Creme-directed video was shot over two nights in Atlanta, GA in November 1983 during the *Synchronicity* tour and is always regarded as one of the best concert videos of the 1980s. The problem is, it's not one of the best despite the music.

The decision to shoot in video led to a dated, very cheesy look to the whole thing and the camerawork and editing are a constant annoyance. The clothes they are wearing – Sting in particular – do not help matters. The performances are excellent, of course, but the backing singers in the drum majorette outfits look equally as ridiculous as the band.

Originally, the show in Montreal, Québec, Canada, from 2 August 1983 was to be used for the video release, but the band felt it wasn't a great show and asked to have another gig filmed, which led to the two Atlanta shows. Apparently, this first concert in Montreal on 2 August was a hastily announced gig at Le Spectrum as a concert for the fan club before they played a sold-out show in Olympic Stadium before over 60,000 fans the next night. Most of the Montreal show has leaked out on the internet and it's a good performance, but the Atlanta shows were indeed better.

In any case, like most concert videos of the day, *Synchronicity Concert* is not a full show and is missing a number of songs. The 2005 DVD release offered four bonus songs with multi-angle shots that did not appear in the original film and these were: 'Synchronicity II', 'Roxanne', 'Invisible Sun' and 'Don't Stand So Close to Me'. Also added were a 1983 tour program reprint and interview footage from the Australian leg in 1984.

A professionally shot show from this era in Oakland, CA, on 10 September 1983 is well worth seeking out and is one of the best shows from the tour, though it does have a time code at the bottom that runs throughout – only a minor distraction, nonetheless.

Outlandos To Synchronicities – A History of The Police Live (1995)

A mix of interviews, backstage footage and concert clips, this is a frustratingly incomplete look at the band live in concert – some songs get cut short and are interrupted. Some of the footage is crappy bootleg level, and some of it is rehashed from the previous releases of *The Police Around the World* and *Synchronicity Concert*. There's also a mimed TV performance included, which is anything but live. A few clips on here are great to see, but this is largely a misfire. There's so much professionally shot concert footage of The Police out there from each tour to not have those performances officially released is criminal.

Every Breath You Take: The Videos (2003)

A DVD update of the 1987 VHS release, this DVD features the band's music video catalogue. The early videos from The Police that were pre-MTV were largely innocuous and were done just to have something for TV – and it shows.

The videos included are: 'Roxanne', 'Can't Stand Losing You', 'Message in a Bottle', 'Walking on the Moon', 'So Lonely', 'Don't Stand So Close to Me' (their first video with any kind of a story or detail), 'De Do Do Do, De Da Da Da', 'Every Little Things She Does Is Magic', 'Invisible Sun', 'Spirits in the Material World', 'Every Breath You Take', 'Wrapped Around Your Finger', 'Synchronicity II' and 'Don't Stand So Close to Me '86'.

A few of these were never shown on MTV, but the majority of them were on the network constantly. Bonus material included the infamous performance on the Old Grey Whistle Test with live takes of 'Can't Stand Losing You' and 'Next to You' and a documentary hosted by Jools Holland called *The Police in Montserrat* from 1981 which includes 'Demolition Man',

'One World (Not Three)', 'Spirits in the Material World' and 'Every Little Thing She Does Is Magic'. The 1983 piece *Studies in Synchronicity* is also included, making this a very worthy DVD to own.

Truth be told, it wasn't until *Synchronicity* and those clips that were directed by Godley & Creme that The Police put any care into their music videos and it's these that still look wonderful. As far as the transfer goes, the videos are a mix of decent and very good and the audio is excellent. A nice bonus feature would've been any of the numerous professionally shot concerts available like Hamburg, Germany from 1980, Passaic, NJ from 1980, Gateshead, UK from 1982 or Oakland, CA from 1983, but those continue to languish in unofficial circles and are easily viewed on YouTube.

Everyone Stares: The Police Inside Out (2006)

This film was put together by Stewart Copeland and edited from his fifty hours of Super 8mm video footage he shot throughout the band's career. Stewart was rarely seen without his camera when The Police were off stage and he really did document an awful lot of things behind the scenes.

The footage can be rough to watch and listen to at times, but some of it is really amusing. The film opens with a slideshow of photos prior to Stewart acquiring his beloved camera. This includes the earliest times of the band's career. The film spends a lot of time with Kim Turner, who was Copeland's friend and the band's tour manager. They embark for America in search of success and eventually return to the UK and Europe to perform at a variety of festivals as their name is starting to grow in the industry.

The huge rise in success is documented, but also shown is the fractious relationship that develops as Sting begins to exert his dominance, bringing in nearly completed songs and now seeking collaboration far less. The film ends with the band headlining the *US Festival* in 1982, so we never actually see the whole *Synchronicity* era.

At 74 minutes, the film goes by fairly quickly, though there are some tedious moments and the rough footage can be a struggle to get through. The movie premiered at the *Sundance Film Festival* in 2006 and was then released on DVD in September of that year. Reviews were a bit mixed from both fans and critics and while it is not a must-see or anything of the sort, there are worse ways to spend 74 minutes and for any Police fan, there are some illuminating moments to watch. Tis cinema verite experience is not for everyone, but if you're a big enough fan of The Police, you should at least check it out.

Certifiable: Live In Buenos Aires (2008)

Only the second live document of a Police concert officially released and the only full show, *Certifiable: Live in Buenos Aires* not only captured the excellence of the band in concert but thanks to the rabid South American fan base, it also captured the essence of the band as a live experience.

The filming took place over two nights at the well-known River Plate Stadium in Buenos Aires, Argentina, on 1 and 2 December 2007 before two sold-out crowds. The concert runs for around 108 minutes and is presented in wide screen with Dolby Surround and Stereo sound. Jim Gable and Ann Kim directed the film, while Robert Orton produced.

The track listing was representative of what the band was performing in late 2007 and featured the following songs in full: 'Message in a Bottle', 'Synchronicity II', 'Walking on the Moon', 'Voices Inside My Head/When the World Is Running Down', You Make the Best of What's Still Around', 'Don't Stand So Close to Me', 'Driven to Tears', 'Hole in My Life', 'Truth Hits Everybody', 'Every Little Thing She Does Is Magic', 'Wrapped Around Your Finger', 'De Do Do Do, De Da Da Da', 'Invisible Sun', 'Walking in Your Footsteps', 'Can't Stand Losing You', 'Reggatta de Blanc', 'Roxanne', 'King of Pain', 'So Lonely', 'Every Breath You Take' and 'Next to You'.

The show is presented on DVD or Blu-Ray and each version includes a bonus two-CD version of the concert, which makes this the only Police live show fully documented as an official release on CD. Remember that the two shows on the 1995 double-CD *Live!* were each missing a few songs. However, since the double-live CD included with *Certifiable* is not a stand-alone release, it is technically not a live album and merely a live video release.

This recording is ample proof of how excellent the reunion shows were. Some fans were displeased that the guys didn't play straight renditions of the songs, but these three musicians were not going to just spit out the hits like a jukebox and bore themselves. The keys were changed in a number of songs, which is common practice for everyone from Elton John to Paul McCartney. The arrangements were changed on a number of songs, allowing space for jamming and improvising. For the most part, the fans were pleased, but you can't win over everyone.

This would seem to be the final stand from The Police and if so, the guys left behind an amazing legacy and a reunion tour that wasn't just a cash grab (though they certainly grabbed an incredible amount of cash for themselves) but a coda to a career of musical creativity and excellence.

Can't Stand Losing You: Surviving The Police (2012)
It was now Andy Summers' turn to chronicle his years with The Police into film and just like Stewart Copeland did, he titled his project after a Police song.

Released in 2012, this film detailed Summers' feelings about his time with the group and what you come away with is the feeling that he wasn't very happy at all and was quite envious/jealous/resentful of Sting. It's really no wonder why the band didn't last any longer than they did.

There are some nice moments where Andy's successful photography career is looked at, but some portions of the film are actually a shade depressing and tedious to get through. At one point, Andy even gripes that The Rolling Stones didn't pick him to replace the late Brian Jones in 1969 and went with Mick Taylor instead. Taylor proved to be an outstanding choice and it's unlikely Andy would've been happy acquiescing with Mick Jagger and Keith Richards if he had issues with Sting.

A lot of this film is based on Andy's book *One Train Later,* so if you've read that, then you know what this is going to be about. This film is still worthwhile because you get to know more about Summers and the early struggles of The Police. Andy details the early days of his photography before The Police and about his days with all the different artists that he played with prior. There are clips of the band live at various points and this goes right up to the reunion tour. It does not appear that Andy was interviewed for anything here and that may be why existing interview clips were used instead. Also, Andy's voice is a bit dry and monotone for the narration, but that's easy to forgive. Also very nice to see is Andy's relationship with his wife Kate, which ended during The Police days in the early 1980s but started again years later and still goes to this day.

While this film is far from perfect, it is fairly enjoyable and well worth watching. In my opinion, it is much better than Stewart's film, though it is a bit unfair to compare the two as they were presented in totally different ways. It's also noteworthy that if it had been up to Andy, The Police never would've ended. This film is recommended for any Police fan, but with slightly tempered expectations.

Released! The Human Rights Concerts 1986-1998 (2013)

This incredible box set was released in 2013 and was the first official release of the various Amnesty International concerts that took place in 1986, 1988, 1990 and 1998, along with various one-off performances by solo performers from 1979-2012 on stage and in the studio for the cause.

Of special note for Police fans was the 1986 Conspiracy of Hope Tour DVD of the East Rutherford, NJ show. Although all eleven hours are not here, quite a lot of it is.

From the 1986 show, full sets on two DVDs are shown from Jackson Browne, The Neville Brothers w/ Joan Baez, Lou Reed, Peter Gabriel, Bryan Adams, U2 and The Police. A few songs each from Third World, The Hooters, Peter, Paul & Mary, Joan Armatrading, Ruben Blades, Yoko Ono, Miles Davis, Howard Jones, Little Steven & The Disciples of Soul, Bob Geldof and Joni Mitchell also appear, though those sets are incomplete.

The Police set is complete and is the major draw here. To have this 1986 performance (in what was at the time the final moment of their career) in total on an official release is a glorious thing indeed. It's all here with 'Message in a Bottle' as the exciting opener and the band also delivering 'King of Pain', 'Driven to Tears', 'Every Breath You Take', 'Roxanne', 'Invisible Sun' and 'I Shall Be Released' with some of the other big names like Bono, Lou Reed, Peter Gabriel and Jackson Browne joining Sting, Stewart and Andy for this emotional finale.

The 1988 DVD features Youssou N'Dour, Tracy Chapman, Peter Gabriel, Bruce Springsteen & the E. Street Band and Sting and runs over three hours, though no set is complete and only a few songs from each act are presented. A real highlight is Springsteen joining Sting and his band to play 'Every Breath You Take'.

The 1990 show is only 70 minutes of highlights with a strange array of artists, including Wynton Marsalis, New Kids on the Block (!), Sinead O'Connor, Ruben Blades, Jackson Browne, Peter Gabriel and once again, Sting. Here, we get a stellar version of Sting and his band doing the Jimi Hendrix classic 'Little Wing'. Documentaries are also included on the 1986, 1988 and 1998 shows on this DVD, which runs over three hours.

Another DVD attached to this one has more documentary footage and two early Amnesty performances from Pete Townshend with classical guitarist John Williams in 1979 and Sting with musicians billed as The Secret Police playing 'I Shall Be Released' in 1981. A variety of songs on stage and in studio from 2007-2012 are also included from different artists.

The 1998 DVD has 150 minutes of the show in Paris, France, from Peter Gabriel with Yossou N'Dour, Alanis Morissette, Asian Dub Foundation, Shania Twain, Kassav', Tracy Chapman, Jimmy Page & Robert Plant, Bruce Springsteen and Radiohead.

All in all, this five-DVD set is brilliant and it is for a fantastic cause that still needs attention today. With the whole 1986 Police set, as well as two different performances from Sting, needless to say, this needs to be owned by Police fans for multiple reasons.

The Police On The Road
Early Live Dates 1977-78

As a live act, The Police began rehearsing in early 1977 and played their first formal gig at Alexander's in Newport, Wales, in the UK on 1 March 1977 as they (Sting and Stewart, that is, not Henry) backed up New York punk/pop singer Cherry Vanilla and played their own set as an opener. When it came time for their own set, The Police played ten songs in seventeen minutes, which was quite punk indeed.

They continued these gigs with Cherry Vanilla until 15 March and then played shows with Wayne County & the Electric Chairs in The Netherlands from 19 March until 27 March and also played a show with Wayne County in Paris, France, on 28 March. A show from 6 March at The Nashville Room is the earliest Police audio recording as some fan was smart enough to capture the band at this stage playing just their fourth show ever – the recording isn't that bad at all. It also proves Henry was anything but incompetent as a guitar player. After that it was back to the UK for more gigs with Cherry Vanilla from 3 April until 11 April, then again from 27 April until 7 May and then an additional two shows in Paris on 12-13 May.

Very crucial was the show as Strontium 90 with Mike Howlett at the Hippodrome in Paris, France, on 28 May, which is the first time that Sting, Stewart and Andy played a full show together. The guys also backed up Howlett under the pseudonym The Elevators two more times on 12 July at Dingwalls in London and on 21 July at The Nashville Room, also in London.

The first headlining show for The Police occurred on 31 May 1977 at the Railway Hotel in London. There were a few scattered shows after that and at a show on 24 June 1977, Andy Summers joined Sting, Stewart and Henry on stage for the encore. Andy would force his way into the band in July and The Police played their first show as a quartet on 25 July 1977 at The Music Machine in London. They would not play again until the festival in Mont-de-Marsan, France, on 5 August, which would be their second and final appearance as a four-piece. There are even brief black-and-white video snippets of this show online and there's a full audio recording – of surprisingly good quality – that was issued as an unofficial release called *Pre-Synchronisms*. The setlist for that show featured 'Landlord', 'Visions of the Night', 'Kids to Blame' (this was a song from Stewart's days with Curved Air), 'Clowns Revenge (Clouds in Venice)', 'Three O'Clock Shit', 'Nothing Achieving', 'It's My Life' (The Animals classic which Andy had played during his tenure with Eric Burdon and the New Animals, although The Police had been playing this with Padovani already), 'Fall Out', 'How Are You', 'Dead End Job' and 'Visions of the Night' for a second time.

On 18 August 1977, The Police played their first show with the lineup of just Sting, Stewart and Andy at Rebecca's in Birmingham, England. A number of dates after that were cancelled and the money wasn't exactly rolling in to begin with. Two shows supporting The Damned occurred in The Netherlands on 16 and 17 of October and it was here on these dates in a hotel where Sting wrote 'Roxanne'. From 28 October until 3 November 1977, The Police backed up Eberhard Schoener for a number of dates in Germany as mentioned earlier.

Once the calendar changed to 1978, the band played a show at The Marquee in London on 22 January 1978 and after a few more dates were scrapped, they played a steady stream of concerts from 9 February until 4 March in the UK and then did three dates supporting psychedelic rockers Spirit later in March and one date opening for reggae act Steel Pulse in April. After that, it was a return to Germany to back up Schoener from 13 May until 27 May. A couple of shows in August saw The Police opening for punk act Chelsea and three more headlining dates followed at The Marquee (9 September), Rock Garden (14 September) and The Nashville Room (3 October). That Nashville Room gig is available to hear in pretty good quality online and is evidence that the talent was above the songs they were playing at this juncture.

Outlandos d'Amour Tour 1978-79
The first national tour from The Police saw them in a Ford Econoline van playing in the US just hours after they landed by plane with nary a soul knowing who in the world they were. The tour began in the US on 20 October 1978 at the infamous CBGB's in New York, NY and ended up concluding on 24 June 1979 in Dortmund, Germany. The Police actually played at CBGB's again the next night (actually around 2:30 am) on 21 October and then drove the van to Philadelphia, PA for a date at the long-defunct club Grendel's Lair on 22 October, playing before approximately 100 fans out of a capacity of 212 – Shea Stadium, this most certainly was not.

Then it was up to Poughkeepsie, NY and, Syracuse, NY and the rock and roll hotbed of Willimantic, CT (yes, that's sarcasm) before playing a four-show stand at The Rat in Boston, MA, from 26-29 October 1978. The date in Poughkeepsie drew less than 75 people and the price of admission was only $2. That was a packed house compared to the show in Willimantic.

That gig was an absolute disaster. Ian Copeland had convinced the owner of the club Shaboo to let The Police play there. The owner only agreed after Copeland promised to have Iggy Pop play a gig there later in the year. This venue wasn't some joke. Other acts that played there shortly after The Police included such names as the Pat Travers Band, Joe Cocker and Todd Rundgren. The Police made a hilarious $12 US dollars that night and Sting wrote a song called 'Goodbye Willimantic', though it was never recorded by the band and was more of a joke than anything else.

The dates continued mainly in the northeast of the US, but also parts of the Midwest and two dates in Canada in Toronto. The dates concluded with two more CBGB's gigs on 14 and 15 November. A return to the UK lasted from 25 November through to 29 December. There were also quite a number of gigs that took place backing up Schoener again from 9 January 1979 until 1 February 1979, including a TV appearance on 18 January in Bremen, Germany.

After a few more UK dates, the band returned to the US and this time, they played all over the country, including the West Coast, which featured a three-night stint at the legendary Whisky A-Go-Go in Los Angeles, CA, from 1 March to 3 March and The Police went down extremely well. By the time they returned to cities like New York, Philadelphia and Boston, they were now playing theatres such as The Bottom Line, Walnut Street Theatre and Paradise Theater, respectively.

A typical setlist on this tour would see the band play the following songs: 'Peanuts', 'The Bed's Too Big Without You', 'No Time This Time', 'Fall Out', 'Hole in My Life', 'Landlord', 'Visions of the Night', 'So Lonely', 'Roxanne', 'Next to You', 'Born in the 50's', 'Be My Girl-Sally', 'Truth Hits Everybody', 'Can't Stand Losing You', 'Next to You' and 'Dead End Job'. As the tour neared the end they would also debut 'Message in a Bottle' and 'Reggatta de Blanc'.

The concerts were high-energy and still had an alignment to punk rock, or at least the punk rock aesthetic, as clearly they were not simply bashing out three-chord angst-filled rockers and were already seriously talented musicians exploring the possibilities of mixing rock, pop and reggae with hints of punk.

The professionally shot performances on this tour included an appearance on the German TV program *Musikladen* on 18 January 1979 in Bremen, Germany, that runs for about 35 minutes and a show from Hatfield Polytechnic on 21 February 1979 filmed for BBC Two's show *Rock Goes to College*, which saw the band play for about 40 minutes or so.

Reggatta De Blanc Tour 1979-80

Now with two albums of material to choose from, The Police expanded their setlists with more songs and less of a reliance on the early punk style, though some of that still seeped in a smidgeon. The tour would start on 17 August 1979 in Bilzen, Belgium and finished up on 28 April 1980 in Newcastle, UK (Sting's birthplace) at City Hall.

The band had already graduated to headlining status, playing theatres in North America and selling those venues out, leaving the club scene behind. On 6 February 1980, they performed live for major US TV network ABC on *Don Kirschner's Rock Concert* in Los Angeles, CA. This tour also saw The Police play Japan for the first time from 14 February until 20 February 1980.

China, Australia, New Zealand, India, Egypt, Greece, Italy, France, Spain, Belgium, The Netherlands, Spain and Canada also enjoyed seeing the band live. Of course, as mentioned earlier, the exotic locales such as Egypt, India and China would be documented in the filmed documentary directed by Derek Burbidge titled *The Police Around the World,* which was released in 1982.

Setlists varied, but songs that appeared at most shows were: 'Next to You', 'So Lonely', 'Walking on the Moon', 'Hole in My Life', 'Deathwish', 'Fall Out', 'Truth Hits Everybody', 'Bring on the Night', 'Visions of the Night', 'Message in a Bottle', 'The Bed's Too Big Without You', 'Peanuts', 'Roxanne', 'Can't Stand Losing You', 'Reggatta de Blanc', 'Landlord', 'Born in the 50's' and 'Be My Girl-Sally'.

Zenyatta Mondatta Tour 1980-81

By the time of this tour, The Police had graduated to arenas and even stadiums on some occasions. They were almost one of the biggest bands in the world, but not quite there yet. The new album *Zenyatta Mondatta* was their biggest seller by far and the larger venues were necessary to satisfy ticket demand. The band were also increasing their musicality on this tour and getting better as musicians despite the exhaustive schedule. The day the band completed recording of the album, they began touring immediately.

The jaunt started on 26 July 1980 at the Milton Keynes Concert Bowl in the UK and ran until 26 February 1981 in Perth, Australia. Countries they played aside from the UK, US and Canada were Australia, New Zealand, Japan, Argentina, Germany, France, Spain, Portugal, Belgium and Ireland. In terms of songs on this leg, the band usually played: 'Voices Inside My Head' (as intro music), 'Don't Stand So Close to Me', 'Walking on the Moon', 'Deathwish', 'Fall Out', 'Man in a Suitcase', 'Bring on the Night', 'De Do Do Do, De Da Da Da', 'Truth Hits Everybody', 'Shadows in the Rain', 'When the World is Running Down, You Make the Best of What's Still Around', 'The Bed's Too Big Without You', 'Driven to Tears', 'Message in a Bottle', 'Roxanne', 'Can't Stand Losing You', 'Reggatta de Blanc', 'Next to You' and 'So Lonely'.

A concert in Bremen, Germany, on 18 October 1980 was filmed for the legendary German TV concert program *Rockpalast,* which can easily be seen on the internet, and a show in Mexico City, Mexico, on 15 November 1980 was partially filmed and interviews were also shot for Mexican television. A US concert in Passaic, NJ, at the Capital Theater on 29 November 1980 was also filmed in black and white and although the footage is a little rough looking and sounding, it's professionally shot by the in-house cameras and is a fantastic gig.

Ghost In The Machine Tour 1981-82

The 1981-82 tour saw the band filling arenas and stadiums around the world and also playing multiple dates in a number of cities due to the crazy ticket demand. It's not just that The Police were a hot ticket; they were considered one of the very best bands to see and had huge crossover appeal to fans of all different kinds of music.

The tour started with four warmup gigs on 29 and 30 July 1981 in Caracas, Venezuela as the band visited there for the first time and two gigs in North

America, one of which was on 22 August 1981 at Liberty Bell Track in Philadelphia, PA which was a site for thoroughbred horse racing that only occasionally had concerts (also on the incredible bill for this show were Oingo Boingo, The Specials, The Go-Go's and of all people, 1950's vocal group The Coasters of 'Yakety Yak' fame), and 23 August 1981 in Oakville, Ontario in Canada.

The tour proper then started on 1 October 1981 in Boblingen, Germany and lasted for nearly a year until 6 September 1982 in Las Cruces, NM, at the Memorial Coliseum. The tour was beyond exhaustive and saw the band play North America three separate times with a winter leg, a spring leg and a summer leg, as well as the UK (where they played three straight sold-out nights at Wembley Arena on 14, 15 and 16 December 1981 just prior to Christmas), Germany, Sweden, Denmark, The Netherlands, France, Brazil, Chile and Italy. The guys would sell out a three-night stand at the Brendan Byrne Arena in East Rutherford, NJ, just outside of New York on 18, 19 and 21 April of 1982. Another three-show sellout run took place in Los Angeles, CA, on 8, 9 and 10 February 1982 at the Great Western Forum.

The Police also played as headliners on the first day of the massive three-day *US Festival* before over 250,000 scorching hot fans in the California desert on 3 September 1982 (the headliners on the other nights were Tom Petty & the Heartbreakers and Fleetwood Mac). The band were paid quite handsomely and put on a full set. It wasn't until recently that this performance finally surfaced online, although it has a timecode on the video, which makes it annoying to watch. Nonetheless, it's great to finally see it after four decades. The *US Festival* was a giant success and failure simultaneously. The festival was organized by Steve Wozniak who had co-founded Apple. The shows took place in the steaming hot California desert in San Bernadino, CA on Labor Day weekend and took place over three days from 3 September to 5 September, with an amazing array of huge acts and great up-and-coming acts being featured. The enormity of the production costs and building the giant stage and sound system, as well as what the artists were paid, made it a huge financial loss of well over £8.5 (or $12 million in US dollars) for the organizers.

The Police put on a fantastic show for well over 90 minutes and played songs from all four albums, with six apiece from the two most recent records *Zenyatta Mondatta* and *Ghost in the Machine*. That day also featured Gang of Four, The Ramones, The Beat (or in the US known as The English Beat), Oingo Boingo, The B-52's and Talking Heads. Other huge acts on the weekend included The Grateful Dead, Santana, The Cars, The Kinks, Jackson Browne and loads of others.

The set for the *Ghost in the Machine* tour usually featured these numbers: 'Voices Inside My Head', 'Message in a Bottle', 'Every Little Thing She Does is Magic', 'Walking on the Moon', 'Spirits in the Material World', 'Hungry for You', 'When the World is Running Down, You Make the Best of What's Still

Around', 'The Bed's Too Big Without You', 'De Do Do Do, De Da Da Da', 'Demolition Man', 'Shadows in the Rain', 'Bring on the Night', 'Driven to Tears', 'One World (Not Three)', 'Invisible Sun', 'Roxanne', 'Don't Stand So Close to Me', 'Can't Stand Losing You', 'Reggatta de Blanc', 'Be My Girl-Sally' and 'So Lonely'.

A few other songs briefly made the set including 'Too Much Information', 'Secret Journey', 'Man in a Suitcase' (only played at two shows), 'Deathwish' (this made it to three gigs), 'Next to You', 'Truth Hits Everybody' and 'Fall Out', which even got two plays on the warm-up dates, while a portion of 'I Burn for You' was a delightful surprise at the *US Festival* performance but was not played anywhere else.

While the shows were uniformly excellent, the three-piece horn section (known as The Chops) was completely unnecessary and only worked well on a few songs. Thankfully they didn't play on all the songs, but it was a bad idea and Sting was responsible. Andy and Stewart were not thrilled with the horns, but obviously had little say in the end.

Aside from the *US Festival* show, professionally shot footage can be seen from this tour from Vina del Mar, Chile, on 20 February 1982 for about an hour (the quality is excellent) and the full show for 90 minutes from Gateshead, UK on 31 July 1982 in great quality as well. Overall, the tour was a smashing financial windfall, but amazingly enough, it wasn't even close to what the next tour would achieve.

Synchronicity Tour 1983-84

There was simply no stopping The Police at this point; the only ones who could stop them would be themselves. The new album *Synchronicity* was a monolith, topping the US album charts for seventeen weeks and selling over eight million copies there and loads more worldwide.

The Police were on the radio and MTV every minute of the day, it seemed and 'Every Breath You take' became one of the biggest songs in music history. Ticket demand for the tour was even larger than before and MTV sponsored the North American tour, plugging it constantly each day on the air.

Technology would now play a role in the music as Sting wanted to use the Oberheim OBX – a synthesizer which would require proper sequencing, programming and extra time. Stewart also had to use technology by programming drum patterns and sequences to play along to what Sting had programmed. Stewart used an Oberheim DMX drum machine for this.

The band had planned to play some warmup gigs, but the equipment wasn't ready and Sting was battling with a sore throat, which knocked him out of commission for a couple of weeks. Tour rehearsals would then take place at Brixton Academy in the UK for a few days before they embarked to America to begin the tour proper on 23 July 1983 with a concert at Comiskey Park in Chicago, IL before close to 50,000 fans.

The tour continued all summer long and an appearance at JFK Stadium in Philadelphia, PA, on 20 August 1983, in front of approximately 70,000 fans in blazing heat, featured Joan Jett & the Blackhearts, Madness and a very young R.E.M. on the bill as well. Other opening acts who appeared on the tour at various times included The Fixx, The Animals, Bryan Adams, UB40, Thompson Twins, Re-Flex, Talking Heads (for one special show) and, for two gigs, Stevie Ray Vaughn & Double Trouble.

The year ended with four consecutive sellouts at Wembley Arena after Christmas that concluded on New Year's Eve, with a few songs being beamed live on MTV via satellite. The first European leg took place in England, Germany, France, Spain, The Netherlands, Denmark and Sweden. A second North American jaunt followed and then it was back to England as well as Scotland and Italy. Another North American leg was then tackled, with that set of dates concluding in Honolulu, HI, on 25 February 1984. The tour finally ended on 4 March 1984 in Melbourne, Australia, at the Melbourne Fairgrounds. The tour had featured six separate legs and a total of 105 concerts.

For the first time in live performances, the band utilized backing vocalists, with Michelle Cobb, Dolette McDonald and Tessa Niles handling the chores. The sequencers were also used during a number of songs, so the musical dynamics on this tour were far different than anything the band had done on stage before. The shows were geared as a heavy mixture of new material and classics from the first four albums. In fact, all but two songs from *Synchronicity* were performed (sorry fans, no 'Mother' performances on this tour). As mentioned above in the video section, shows in Atlanta, GA, in November 1983 were filmed for the release of the concert video *Synchronicity Tour* and several other shows from the tour can be seen online that were professionally shot, including a fantastic show in Oakland, CA on 10 September 1983 and the show in Montreal, Quebec in Canada that was not used for the concert video.

Generally speaking, these were the songs that made the cut for this tour: 'Voices Inside My Head', 'Synchronicity I', 'Synchronicity II', 'Message in a Bottle', 'Walking on the Moon', 'O My God', 'De Do Do Do, De Da Da Da', 'Wrapped Around Your Finger', 'Tea in the Sahara', 'Spirits in the Material World', 'Hole in My Life', 'Invisible Sun', 'One World (Not Three)', 'King of Pain', 'Every Breath You Take', 'Murder by Numbers', 'Don't Stand So Close to Me', 'Roxanne', 'Can't Stand Losing You', 'Reggatta de Blanc' and 'So Lonely'. Songs that seldom appeared included: 'Demolition Man', 'Next to You' and rather surprisingly 'Every Little Thing She Does is Magic'. The aftermath of the tour saw The Police with nothing left to achieve. They'd done it all and they'd conquered the world. Sting wanted to begin his solo career and Stewart and Andy both had an interest in photography and film scores. There was never any official announcement, but rumours began spreading over the next few years that The Police had disbanded. This wasn't quite true, but it wouldn't be long before that sad fact became reality.

Sting was quoted years later saying something very telling about this tour after the Shea Stadium gig:

I realized that you can't get better than this, you can't climb a mountain higher than this. This is Everest. I made the decision on stage that ok, this is it, this is where this thing stops, right now.

Amnesty International Conspiracy Of Hope Tour 1986

Sting was one of the performers on the Amnesty International tour *Conspiracy of Hope* in 1986 which was a two-week jaunt across the US to raise awareness of human rights violations in nations around the world, particularly political prisoners. The shows took place in June of 1986 and concluded with a massive show at Giants Stadium in East Rutherford, NJ on 15 June 1986, a *Live Aid*-type event that was an eleven-hour concert starting at noon and ending at 11pm.

The whole show was broadcast live on MTV and the network learned its lesson from the mistakes of its terrible *Live Aid* coverage by not skipping any songs or talking over performances, or worse, leaving live performances for commercials, as the US coverage had been, although coverage in the UK was far better. The concert was far more diverse culturally and musically than *Live Aid* and featured an incredible bill. The headliners all played exactly 30 minutes apiece and other acts played anywhere from one to three songs each.

Acts from all parts of the musical world were on the bill and included John Eddy, Peter, Paul & Mary, Stanley Jordan, Joan Armatrading, Ruben Blades, Yoko Ono, Howard Jones, Bob Geldof, Carlos Santana, Fela Kuti and Joni Mitchell. The headlining acts were Bryan Adams, The Hooters, Jackson Browne, Lou Reed, Little Steven & the Disciples of Soul, Third World, The Neville Brothers with Joan Baez, Miles Davis, Peter Gabriel, U2 and... The Police.

The Police decided to play the last three shows of the tour, beginning in Atlanta, GA on 11 June, then Chicago, IL, on 13 June and the East Rutherford concert on 15 June. The guys sounded as if they'd never been away and were very tight and committed to the cause, hence a set with largely topical songs such as 'Driven to Tears' and 'Invisible Sun' (which they played with Bono of U2 handling some vocals each night).

Kenny Kirkland from Sting's band played keyboards on these shows and the extra textures really emboldened the sound, making these concerts all the better. The arrangements were tight, but the playing was still very creative, with Stewart attacking his drum kit as he always had and Andy really lashing out a wicked solo on 'Driven to Tears' each night. Sting's bass playing and singing were as good as always and it's actually quite sad that we only received these three performances in 1986. It's a blessing that these performances even happened though and right from the first show in Atlanta, the boys were ready.

The Atlanta show was the first the band had done since March 1984 in Australia. They played 'Spirits in the Material World', 'King of Pain', 'Driven to Tears', 'Wrapped Around Your Finger', 'Every Breath You Take', 'Roxanne' and 'Message in a Bottle'. The crowd went ballistic when The Police took the stage and continued to give the band raucous applause throughout. Atlanta of course was also the site of the filming of the *Synchronicity Concert* video.

The next show in Chicago drew even bigger reactions from the audience, and at this gig, they opened with 'Message in a Bottle' (instead of closing with it) and added 'Invisible Sun' as well as the finale of Bob Dylan's 'I Shall Be Released' where they were joined by other big names from the evening. This show was even better than Atlanta was.

And then things culminated with the East Rutherford performance which was shown live around the world thanks to MTV. After a nearly twelve-hour day of incredible acts, The Police finished the steaming hot day off and delivered the goods with 'Message in a Bottle' restored as the opener, followed by 'King of Pain', 'Driven to Tears', 'Every Breath You Take', 'Roxanne', 'Invisible Sun' and 'I Shall Be Released'.

It is telling that, as the band finished their set and the Dylan song began, the guys handed their instruments to U2 almost as if they were passing on the mantle. Bono even said in an interview with *Rolling Stone*: 'It was very emotional for them. I think it was clear in Sting's eyes that he was not going to be in a band anymore. They had come together for this tour and that was it'.

As we know, the band did head into the studio to do a new album, but the results were a disaster, and these three performances were to be the last from The Police for over two decades – though nobody knew that at the time. Did Sting truly know that these were the last shows The Police would perform until reuniting in 2007? There did seem to be a sense of it on his face, but you couldn't tell by the actual playing of the music as the band sounded outstanding once again.

The Reunion Tour 2007-08

By 2007, it had finally happened. The moment all fans had been dreaming of for decades was now becoming a surprising reality.

News had leaked out that The Police were reuniting for a monstrous tour that would last a year from 2007-2008. On 11 February 2007, the band performed 'Roxanne' at the Grammys in Los Angeles, CA and followed that up with a special club gig at the Whisky A-Go-Go in Los Angeles on 12 February, playing a five-song set. They then began rehearsing for a few months shortly thereafter. The tour would kick off in Vancouver, British Columbia in Canada, at the GM Place before crowds of 30,000 plus, with two sold-out shows on 27 and 28 May that thrilled the fans. Every show in the US and UK was sold out, with the band filling stadiums, often playing to over 40,000-50,000 a night. The whole British tour sold out in just 30 minutes! The largest crowd was over 82,000 in Dublin, Ireland and dates in Japan, Australia, New Zealand and South America were also played before enormous crowds. The Police played everywhere, from Singapore to Puerto Rico and beyond.

Tied into the tour was a release of a double-CD compilation called *The Police*, which hit number three in the UK and went Platinum, also going gold in Canada and reaching number eleven on the US charts, selling well throughout the world. This was also the first compilation to include the band's debut single 'Fall Out', which was celebrating its 30th birthday that year, as were The Police as a band.

The set had a number of songs remain stagnant, but there were plenty of changes during the tour as some songs had rare appearances and others popped up and remained. They also slipped in a few covers here and there. The shows were magnificent and the band changed some of the keys and arrangements on certain songs while sticking to the originals on the others. There were also extended jams on some cuts, with Andy unleashing a furious, extended solo on 'Driven to Tears' for example. A typical setlist was 'Message in a Bottle', 'Walking on the Moon', 'Demolition Man', 'Voices in My Head', 'When the World is Running Down, You make the Best of What's Still Around', 'Don't Stand So Close to Me', 'Driven to Tears', 'Hole in My Life', 'Every Little Thing She Does Is Magic', 'Wrapped Around Your Finger', 'De Do Do Do, De Da Da Da', 'Invisible Sun', 'Can't Stand Losing You', 'Reggatta de Blanc', 'Roxanne', 'King of Pain', 'So Lonely', 'Every Breath You Take' and 'Next to You'.

The tour did feature other songs at times as they wisely decided against a static setlist and these selections were also performed: 'Synchronicity II', 'Walking in Your Footsteps', 'Truth Hits Everybody', 'The Bed's Too Big Without You', 'Spirits in the Material World', 'Dead End Job', 'Murder by Numbers' and 'Bring on the Night'.

On 7 July 2007, during the first leg of the tour in North America, the band played at the East Rutherford, NJ portion of the global *Live Earth* concerts, which were a direct knock-off of the *Live Aid* concerts organized by Al Gore to raise awareness about environmental concerns and global warming. The Police were headliners of the East Rutherford show, which also featured big names like Bon Jovi, Smashing Pumpkins, Roger Waters, Alicia Keys, Kayne West and the Dave Matthews Band. The Police played a five-song set to end the concert, including 'Driven to Tears', 'Roxanne', 'Can't Stand Losing You', 'Reggatta de Blanc' and for 'Message in a Bottle' – the final song in their set – they were joined by John Mayer on guitar and Kanye West. Kanye sure as hell had no idea what he was doing or had any semblance of the lyrics. Somebody must've lost a bet to allow this debacle to happen, but John Mayer added class with his playing and singing. At least it was for a good cause. The Police performing 'Driven to Tears' is on the official *Live Earth* DVD release, though no other songs were included.

As the reunion tour went along, spirits remained high and each show was special. On 29 and 30 September 2007 in Paris, original guitarist Henry Padovani joined the band on stage for a rousing take of 'Next to You', which was wonderful to see and had everyone smiling. The tour came to a close on 7 August 2008 at Madison Square Garden in New York City, NY and this was an emotional show – it truly was to be the last one. They opened with a scorching cover of Cream's 'Sunshine of Your Love' and then performed 'Message in a Bottle' with the New York City Drum & Bugle Corps. Later, they would also cover the Jimi Hendrix Experience classic 'Purple Haze'. The final song they would ever play was 'Next to You'.

The reunion tour went from 27 May 2007 until that final show in New York on 7 August 2008. Attendance was at a mind-boggling 98% of all tickets available. Besides the US, Canada and the UK, the guys also tore through Japan, Sweden, Denmark, Germany, The Netherlands, Switzerland, Austria, Portugal, Spain, France, Italy, Ireland, Belgium, Wales, Mexico, Argentina, Chile, Brazil, Australia, New Zealand, Singapore, China, Northern Ireland, Poland and Puerto Rico.

Nepotism saw Sting's son Joe Sumner and his band Fiction Plane opening along with The Fratellis in 2007. The Foo Fighters (in Los Angeles) and Maroon 5 (in Miami) were big names that hopped on for a show each, as did Beck for one gig in Chile. Fergie opened on all the shows in Oceania (Australia and New Zealand). For all of the 2008 concerts in North America, fans were treated to Elvis Costello & the Imposters, while 2008 gigs in Europe featured Starsailor for a few gigs, as well as The Charlatans and Counting Crows, who played on one show. For the final show ever in New York, The B-52's were special guests.

When all was said and done, the tour grossed a stunning £252.9 million ($358 million) on close to four million tickets sold. On 11 November 2008, as mentioned earlier, a double live DVD, which also included two CDs, was released under the title *Certifiable: Live in Buenos Aires,* which also included a bonus DVD filmed by Copeland's son, Jordan, called *Better Than Therapy*, a behind the scenes look at the tour. The set went platinum in the US.

Aside from the official release of *Certifiable*, there are also several other professionally filmed shows to check out from this tour and they are each outstanding. One concert was filmed in full at Maracanã Stadium in Rio de Janeiro, Brazil, on 8 October 2007 and is highly recommended. Another night captured by the cameras was in Tokyo, Japan, at the massive Tokyo Dome on 14 February 2008. There is also a show from the *Rock in Rio* festival on 5 July 2008 in Madrid, Spain, from a date near the end of the tour that is truly fantastic, with the audience beyond enthusiastic.

Prior to the end of the tour, Sting and the band said that this was definitely it and fans should be happy that it even happened. Sting told the media: 'There will be no new album, no big new tour. Once we're done with our reunion tour, that's it for The Police'.

I will let Stewart Copeland sum it all up as only he could:

We made great records, despite the fact it wasn't very comfortable to make them. It's only now that we understand what our conflict was about and acknowledge that everyone's point of view was valid. And we had a very strong work ethic. Nobody ever shirked, nobody stayed at home. All three of us were always leaning forward – and that's the personality in each of us that led to the conflict: one person was anointed the god of all music, while the other two were still pushy sons of bitches. In amongst all that tension, there was always a positive attempt to make it work.

References and Bibliography

There were some very helpful sources as I compiled data and information for this book that I was able to utilize. These websites proved quite useful, although in a few cases, I had to verify that the information I was using was correct:

www.thepolicewiki.org
www.thepolice.com
www.rollingstone.com
www.sting.com
www.andysummers.com
www.stewartcopeland.net
www.henrypadovani.com
www.setlistfm.com
www.concertarchives.org/bands/the-police
www.amnestyusa.org
www.songfacts.com

I also utilized some information from these print sources:

Betts, G. *The Official Seventies Hits Book* (Official UK Charts Company, 2019)
Betts, G. *The Official Eighties Hits Book* (Official UK Charts Company, 2019)
Fricke, David. 'The Police: A Fragile Truce'. *Rolling Stone*, January 22, 2015
Sting, *Lyrics by Sting* (Dial Press, 2007)
Sutcliffe, Phil. 'Three Man Army'. *Mojo*, issue 165, August 2007, pages 83-97.
Whitburn, J. *Rock Tracks 1981-2020* (Record Research Inc., 2021)
Whitburn, J. *Top Pop Albums 1955-2016* (Record Research Inc., 2018)
Whitburn, J. *Top Pop Singles 1955-2018* (Record Research Inc., 2019)
Copeland, S *The Police Diaries* (Rocket 88, 2023)

Would you like to write for Sonicbond Publishing?

At Sonicbond Publishing we are always on the look-out for authors, particularly for our two main series:

On Track. Mixing fact with in depth analysis, the On Track series examines the work of a particular musical artist or group. All genres are considered from easy listening and jazz to 60s soul to 90s pop, via rock and metal.

On Screen. This series looks at the world of film and television. Subjects considered include directors, actors and writers, as well as entire television and film series. As with the On Track series, we balance fact with analysis.

While professional writing experience would, of course, be an advantage the most important qualification is to have real enthusiasm and knowledge of your subject. First-time authors are welcomed, but the ability to write well in English is essential.

Sonicbond Publishing has distribution throughout Europe and North America, and all books are also published in E-book form. Authors will be paid a royalty based on sales of their book.

Further details are available from www.sonicbondpublishing.co.uk. To contact us, complete the contact form there or email info@sonicbondpublishing.co.uk